# QUICK SOUPS, SIMPLE SALADS

SPECIAL EDITION FOR THE
COOKING CLUB OF AMERICA®
COOKING ARTS COLLECTION™

# QUICK SOUPS, SIMPLE SALADS

### COOKING ARTS COLLECTION™

**Better Homes and Gardens® Books**
**An imprint of Meredith® Books**

Editors: Jennifer Darling, Kristi Fuller
Contributing Editors: Connie Hay, Jane Hemminger,
 Linda Henry, Nancy Hughes, Susan Parenti, Marty Schiel,
 Judy Vance, Mary Williams, Spectrum Communication Services Inc.
Writers: Margaret Agnew, Allison Engel
Designer: Craig Hanken
Copy Chief: Catherine Hamrick
Copy and Production Editor: Terri Fredrickson
Contributing Copy Editor: Marcia Gilmer
Contributing Proofreaders: Gretchen Kauffman,
 Susie Kling, Kathleen Poole, Margaret Smith
Electronic Production Coordinator: Paula Forest
Editorial and Design Assistants: Judy Bailey,
 Mary Lee Gavin, Karen Schirm
Test Kitchen Director: Sharon Stilwell
Test Kitchen Product Supervisors: Colleen Weeden, Jill Hoefler
Food Stylists: Lynn Blanchard, Dianna Nolin, Janet Pittman
Photographers: Jim Krantz, Kritsada Panichgul
Prop Stylists: Nancy Wall Hopkins, Karen Johnson
Production Director: Douglas M. Johnston
Production Manager: Pam Kvitne
Assistant Prepress Manager: Marjorie J. Schenkelberg

**Meredith® Books**
Editor in Chief: James D. Blume
Design Director: Matt Strelecki
Managing Editor: Gregory H. Kayko
Director, Sales & Marketing, Retail: Michael A. Peterson
Director, Sales & Marketing, Special Markets: Rita McMullen
Director, Sales & Marketing, Home & Garden Center Channel:
 Ray Wolf
Director, Operations: George A. Susral

Vice President, General Manager: Jamie L. Martin

***Better Homes and Gardens*® Magazine**
Editor in Chief: Jean LemMon
Executive Food Editor: Nancy Byal

**Meredith Publishing Group**
President, Publishing Group: Christopher M. Little
Vice President, Consumer Marketing
 & Development: Hal Oringer

**Meredith Corporation**
Chairman and Chief Executive Officer: William T. Kerr

Chairman of the Executive Committee: E. T. Meredith III

Originally published as *Better Homes and Gardens® Fresh
and Simple*™ *Quick-Toss Salad Meals* and *Fresh and Simple*™
*Quick-Simmering Soups.*

First Edition. Printing Number and Year: 10 9 8 7 6 5 4 3 2 1
ISBN: 978-1-118-06679-9

# contents

# contents

# great bowls of soup!

Craving soup, but short on time? Doesn't matter. You can still enjoy a bowl of homemade soup in a snap—any day of the week, any time of the year.

*Quick-Simmering Soups* features 65 recipes that stir up fast. Choose from an array of light, warm-weather soups and hearty, cool-weather soups, including updated classics, ethnic favorites, chowders, and easy gourmet soups. This collection also helps you cut down on kitchen detail because most recipes require just one or two pans. Another bonus: Soup is often a meal in itself. Add a salad and warm, crusty bread—and soup's on!

soups for
the soul

# allspice meatball stew

The exotic flavor of this hearty stew comes from the allspice berry of the pimiento tree. Allspice, which can be purchased whole or ground, gets its name because it tastes like a combination of cinnamon, nutmeg, and cloves.

9

**Start to finish: 30 minutes   Makes 8 servings (10 cups)**

In a Dutch oven combine the meatballs, green beans, carrots, beef broth, Worcestershire sauce, allspice, and cinnamon. Bring to boiling; reduce heat. Simmer, covered, for 10 minutes.

Stir in undrained tomatoes. Return to boiling; reduce heat. Simmer, covered, about 5 minutes more or until vegetables are crisp-tender.

Nutrition facts per serving: 233 cal., 13 g total fat (6 g sat. fat), 37 mg chol., 938 mg sodium, 18 g carbo., 4 g fiber, 12 g pro. Daily values: 86% vit. A, 22% vit. C, 5% calcium, 13% iron

*Note: This soup freezes well. Freeze 1-, 2-, or 4-serving portions in sealed freezer containers. To reheat, place frozen soup in a large saucepan. Heat, covered, over medium heat about 30 minutes, stirring occasionally to break apart.*

1 16-ounce package frozen prepared Italian-style meatballs

3 cups green beans cut into 2-inch pieces or frozen cut green beans

2 cups packaged peeled baby carrots

1 14½-ounce can beef broth

2 teaspoons Worcestershire sauce

½ to ¾ teaspoon ground allspice

½ teaspoon ground cinnamon

2 14½-ounce cans stewed tomatoes

# easy cassoulet

The French know cassoulet as a classic, long-simmered dish consisting of white beans and various meats—sausages, pork, or goose. This version is a less time-consuming spin on the classic.

2 14½-ounce cans reduced-sodium chicken broth

2 stalks celery, chopped

2 medium carrots, chopped

1 large onion, chopped

3 cloves garlic, minced

2 teaspoons snipped fresh rosemary

2 15-ounce cans white kidney (cannellini) or navy beans, drained and rinsed

8 ounces cooked smoked turkey sausage links, halved lengthwise and sliced

1 cup chopped cooked chicken

½ cup dry white wine or reduced-sodium chicken broth

2 teaspoons snipped fresh thyme

**Start to finish: 35 minutes    Makes 4 servings (7 cups)**

In a large saucepan combine chicken broth, celery, carrots, onion, garlic, and rosemary. Bring to boiling; reduce heat. Simmer, uncovered, about 5 minutes or until vegetables are tender.

Stir in the beans, turkey sausage, chicken, wine, and thyme. Return to boiling; reduce heat. Simmer, covered, for 5 minutes more.

Nutrition facts per serving: 387 cal., 12 g total fat (3 g sat. fat), 70 mg chol., 1,335 mg sodium, 43 g carbo., 13 g fiber, 35 g pro. Daily values: 119% vit. A, 11% vit. C, 11% calcium, 29% iron

# sausage & vegetable soup

Packaged shredded cabbage mix reduces the prep time and adds convenience for this hearty soup. Smoked sausage and sweet potato contribute new flavor dimensions.

**Start to finish: 35 minutes   Makes 4 servings (6½ cups)**

In a large saucepan cook sausage, onion, and celery over medium heat about 3 minutes or until vegetables are nearly tender. Stir in water, sweet potato, lima beans, pepper, and salt.

Bring to boiling; reduce heat. Simmer, covered, about 15 minutes or until vegetables are just tender. Stir in undrained tomatoes, cabbage mix, and basil. Return to boiling; reduce heat. Simmer, covered, for 2 minutes more.

Nutrition facts per serving: 215 cal., 7 g total fat (2 g sat. fat), 41 mg chol., 624 mg sodium, 28 g carbo., 7 g fiber, 14 g pro. Daily values: 110% vit. A, 75% vit. C, 9% calcium, 16% iron

- 8 ounces cooked smoked turkey sausage links, halved lengthwise and sliced
- 1 medium onion, halved lengthwise and sliced
- 1 stalk celery, sliced
- 3 cups water
- 1 cup chopped peeled sweet potato
- 1 cup frozen lima beans
- ¼ teaspoon pepper
- ⅛ teaspoon salt
- 1 14½-ounce can tomatoes, cut up
- 1½ cups packaged shredded cabbage with carrot (cole slaw mix) or 1½ cups shredded cabbage
- 2 tablespoons snipped fresh basil

# pork & hominy stew

This savory combination could be described as a posole—a thick, hearty Mexican soup traditionally served as a main course at Christmas. Sprinkle shredded radishes over the top for a festive presentation.

12 ounces boneless pork strips for stir-frying

1 large onion, chopped

2 cloves garlic, minced

1 tablespoon cooking oil

4 cups chicken broth

2 medium carrots, thinly sliced

¼ teaspoon ground cumin

¼ teaspoon crushed red pepper

1 14½-ounce can hominy, drained

3 tablespoons snipped fresh cilantro

¼ cup shredded radishes

**Start to finish: 30 minutes   Makes 4 servings (6 cups)**

In a large saucepan cook pork, onion, and garlic in hot oil until pork is slightly pink in center. Remove pork mixture from saucepan; set aside. Add chicken broth, carrots, cumin, and pepper to saucepan.

Bring to boiling; reduce heat. Simmer, covered, about 8 minutes or until carrots are just tender. Add hominy, cilantro, and pork mixture; cook and stir until heated through. Top each serving with radishes.

Nutrition facts per serving: 290 cal., 12 g total fat (3 g sat. fat), 39 mg chol., 1,056 mg sodium, 26 g carbo., 3 g fiber, 20 g pro. Daily values: 118% vit. A, 8% vit. C, 4% calcium, 15% iron

# moroccan lamb tagine

Lamb's richness pairs well with both spices and fruits, particularly the gingerroot, apples, and raisins called for here. If you have saffron on hand, add it for extra flavor and a brighter color. Serve this comforting soup with basmati or wild rice.

**13**

**Start to finish: 35 minutes   Makes 4 servings (7 cups)**

In a large saucepan cook ground lamb, onion, and garlic until lamb is no longer pink. Drain well. Stir in the water, chicken broth, cilantro, gingerroot, pepper, paprika, and, if desired, saffron. Bring to boiling; reduce heat. Simmer, covered, for 10 minutes.

Stir in the apples or pears and raisins or dates. Return to boiling; reduce heat. Simmer, uncovered, for 1 to 2 minutes more or until apples are just slightly softened.

Nutrition facts per serving: 261 cal., 12 g total fat (5 g sat. fat), 57 mg chol., 381 mg sodium, 20 g carbo., 2 g fiber, 18 g pro. Daily values: 1% vit. A, 10% vit. C, 3% calcium, 11% iron

| | |
|---|---|
| 12 | ounces lean ground lamb |
| 1 | large onion, chopped |
| 3 | cloves garlic, minced |
| 2 | cups water |
| 1 | 14½-ounce can chicken broth |
| ½ | cup snipped fresh cilantro |
| 1 | tablespoon grated gingerroot |
| ¼ | teaspoon pepper |
| ¼ | teaspoon paprika |
| ⅛ | teaspoon thread saffron, crushed, or dash ground saffron (optional) |
| 2 | medium apples or pears, cored and thinly sliced |
| ¼ | cup raisins or snipped pitted dates |

## saffron

The spice called saffron comes from the stigmas or threadlike filaments of the purple crocus flower. Each flower contains only three stigmas, which are hand-picked and dried. It takes over 14,000 stigmas to provide an ounce of saffron. Because of the labor intensive process of harvesting the stigmas, saffron is very expensive. You only need a small amount to flavor your recipes, though—a little will go a long way. Saffron comes in thin threads. To release the flavor, crush the threads by rubbing them between your fingers.

# greek minestrone

Arborio rice is an Italian-grown grain that is shorter and plumper than any other short-grain rice. Traditionally used to make creamy risotto, it adds a similar texture to this bean and vegetable soup.

2 stalks celery, finely chopped

1 large onion, finely chopped

2 cloves garlic, minced

1 tablespoon olive oil

5 cups beef broth

1 cup water

½ cup uncooked Arborio rice

6 cups torn spinach

1 15-ounce can great northern beans, drained and rinsed

3 medium tomatoes, chopped (about 2 cups)

1 medium zucchini, coarsely chopped (about 1½ cups)

¼ cup snipped fresh thyme

¼ teaspoon cracked black pepper

½ cup crumbled feta cheese (2 ounces)

**Start to finish: 40 minutes   Makes 6 servings (10½ cups)**

In a Dutch oven cook celery, onion, and garlic in hot oil until tender. Add beef broth, water, and rice. Bring to boiling; reduce heat. Simmer, covered, for 15 minutes.

Add the torn spinach, beans, tomatoes, zucchini, thyme, and pepper. Cook and stir until heated through. Top each serving with feta cheese.

Nutrition facts per serving: 252 cal., 6 g total fat (2 g sat. fat), 8 mg chol., 834 mg sodium, 39 g carbo., 8 g fiber, 13 g pro.  Daily values:  44% vit. A, 58% vit. C, 15% calcium, 31% iron

## the **best** broths

When a recipe calls for chicken, beef, or vegetable broth, you can use a homemade stock recipe or substitute commercially canned broth. Just remember that the canned varieties usually are saltier than homemade stocks, so hold off on adding extra salt until the end of cooking. Then, season to taste. Another option is to try a canned reduced-sodium broth. Bouillon cubes and granules diluted according to package directions may be used, but they are also saltier than homemade stocks.

# chunky ratatouille stew

Simmer the pleasures of a summer garden into this stew. Like typical ratatouille, it combines eggplant, tomatoes, onion, green sweet pepper, and green beans or zucchini. For a fun presentation, serve in hollowed eggplant halves.

**17**

**Start to finish: 35 minutes   Makes 4 servings (6 cups)**

In a Dutch oven cook the onion and green pepper in hot oil until tender. Stir in the mushrooms, eggplant, and green beans. Add beef broth and wine.

Bring to boiling; reduce heat. Simmer, covered, for 8 to 10 minutes or until vegetables are tender. Stir in undrained tomatoes and basil; heat through. Sprinkle each serving with provolone cheese.

Nutrition facts per serving: 163 cal., 8 g total fat (3 g sat. fat), 10 mg chol., 955 mg sodium, 16 g carbo., 3 g fiber, 8 g pro. Daily values: 13% vit. A, 65% vit. C, 14% calcium, 10% iron

1 large onion, chopped

1 cup chopped green sweet pepper

1 tablespoon olive oil

2 cups small whole fresh mushrooms (about 6 ounces), stems removed

2 cups peeled and chopped eggplant (about 6 ounces)

4 ounces green beans, cut into 1-inch pieces, or 1 small zucchini, thinly sliced (about 1 cup)

2 cups beef broth

2 tablespoons dry red wine

1 14½-ounce can diced tomatoes with roasted garlic and red pepper

1 tablespoon snipped fresh basil

½ cup shredded provolone cheese (2 ounces)

# wild rice, barley, & mushroom soup

It's hard to resist this enticing soup. The nutty flavor and chewy texture of wild rice and barley make pleasant contrasts to the earthy flavor and soft texture of the mushrooms. Add a splash of Madeira for a sophisticated accent.

18

1 cup water

¼ cup quick-cooking barley

3 medium leeks, washed, trimmed, and thinly sliced

1 medium carrot, sliced

1 small parsnip, finely chopped

1 clove garlic, minced

1 tablespoon margarine or butter

3 cups sliced fresh mushrooms (about 8 ounces)

1 tablespoon snipped fresh sage or 1 teaspoon dried sage, crushed

2½ cups vegetable broth

¾ cup cooked wild rice

2 tablespoons Madeira wine or dry sherry (optional)

Salt

Pepper

**Start to finish: 25 minutes    Makes 3 servings (5 cups)**

In a small saucepan combine water and barley. Bring mixture to boiling; reduce heat. Simmer, covered, for 10 minutes.

Meanwhile, in a large saucepan cook leeks, carrot, parsnip, and garlic in hot margarine or butter for 5 minutes. Stir in the mushrooms and dried sage (if using). Cook 5 to 10 minutes more or just until mushrooms are tender. Stir in the vegetable broth, cooked wild rice, and, if desired, Madeira. If using, stir in fresh sage. Cook and stir until heated through. Season to taste with salt and pepper.

Nutrition facts per serving: 223 cal., 6 g total fat (1 g sat. fat), 0 mg chol., 854 mg sodium, 45 g carbo., 9 g fiber, 7 g pro.  Daily values:  60% vit. A, 20% vit. C, 5% calcium, 24% iron

**mushroom** know-how
Store fresh mushrooms in the refrigerator. Instead of an airtight container, use a cotton bag or a brown paper sack that will let them breathe. Avoid soaking or washing mushrooms prior to storage; they will absorb water and deteriorate more quickly. Just before using the mushrooms, clean them by wiping with a damp cloth or paper towel.

# potato soup
## with **blue** cheese

The happy marriage of potatoes and blue cheese makes for an idyllic wintry soup. The potatoes promise creamy texture; the cheese pledges robust flavor. Added just before serving, vibrant tomato lends color and freshness.

**19**

**Start to finish: 35 minutes   Makes 3 servings (4 cups)**

In a medium saucepan combine potatoes, water, onion, bouillon granules, and pepper. Bring to boiling; reduce heat. Simmer, covered, about 20 minutes or until potatoes are tender. Mash potatoes slightly; do not drain.

Meanwhile, in a screw-top jar combine ½ cup of the milk and the flour; cover and shake well. Add to saucepan; add the remaining milk. Cook and stir until thickened and bubbly. Cook and stir for 1 minute more.

Add the blue cheese and parsley; stir until the cheese melts. Top each serving with tomato and green onion.

Nutrition facts per serving: 289 cal., 7 g total fat (4 g sat. fat), 21 mg chol., 829 mg sodium, 46 g carbo., 3 g fiber, 12 g pro. Daily values: 15% vit. A, 36% vit. C, 23% calcium, 8% iron

3  medium potatoes, peeled and
   chopped (about 2 cups)

1  cup water

1  small onion, chopped

2  teaspoons instant chicken
   bouillon granules

⅛  teaspoon pepper

2  cups milk

2  tablespoons all-purpose flour

¼  cup crumbled blue cheese
   (1 ounce)

2  tablespoons snipped fresh parsley

½  cup finely chopped tomato

2  tablespoons thinly sliced
   green onion

# curried lentil soup

Humble lentils step out in spicy style with a flavor kick of gingerroot, curry powder, cumin, and cilantro. If you like, a spoonful of sour cream swirled into the soup adds a complementary richness.

6  cups reduced-sodium chicken broth

1½  cups thinly sliced green onions

2  medium carrots, chopped

1  cup dried brown lentils, drained and rinsed

1  tablespoon grated gingerroot

1  teaspoon curry powder

1  teaspoon ground cumin

⅛  to ¼ teaspoon ground red pepper

¼  cup snipped fresh cilantro

½  cup dairy sour cream (optional)

Fresh cilantro sprigs or green onions (optional)

**Start to finish: 40 minutes   Makes 4 servings (6 cups)**

In a large saucepan combine the chicken broth, green onions, carrots, lentils, gingerroot, curry powder, cumin, and red pepper. Bring mixture to boiling; reduce heat. Simmer, covered, for 25 to 30 minutes or until lentils are tender.

Stir in the snipped cilantro; cook for 1 minute more. If desired, top each serving with sour cream and garnish with cilantro sprigs.

Nutrition facts per serving: 201 cal., 3 g total fat (0 g sat. fat), 0 mg chol., 986 mg sodium, 32 g carbo., 3 g fiber, 15 g pro. Daily values: 88% vit. A, 16% vit. C, 4% calcium, 36% iron

# asparagus & cheese
## potato soup

A treasure of spring—tender, purple-tinged asparagus—is featured in this soup. Sour cream lends a tangy flavor to this creamy delight.

**Start to finish: 35 minutes    Makes 4 servings (5½ cups)**

In a large saucepan cook onion in hot oil until tender. Sprinkle flour over onion and stir to coat. Add the asparagus, milk, chicken broth, potatoes, salt, and red pepper.

Cook and stir until thickened and bubbly; reduce heat. Simmer, covered, for 10 to 12 minutes or until vegetables are just tender, stirring occasionally. Add cheddar cheese, tomato, and sour cream; stir until cheese melts.

Nutrition facts per serving: 383 cal., 21 g total fat (11 g sat. fat), 48 mg chol., 730 mg sodium, 31 g carbo., 3 g fiber, 18 g pro. Daily values: 28% vit. A, 56% vit. C, 34% calcium, 15% iron

1 large onion, chopped

4 teaspoons cooking oil

3 tablespoons all-purpose flour

2 cups 1-inch pieces asparagus spears or broccoli flowerets

2 cups milk

1 14½-ounce can chicken broth

8 ounces red potatoes, cubed (about 1½ cups)

¼ teaspoon salt

⅛ teaspoon ground red pepper

1 cup shredded sharp cheddar cheese (4 ounces)

1 small tomato, seeded and chopped

⅓ cup dairy sour cream

# black & white bean chili

Calling all hearty appetites! This satisfying blend of black beans, white kidney beans, jicama, and chile peppers boasts a pronounced south-of-the-border flavor.

1 medium onion, chopped

1 clove garlic, minced

1 tablespoon cooking oil

1 15-ounce can white kidney (cannellini) beans, drained and rinsed

1 15-ounce can black beans, drained and rinsed

1 14½-ounce can chicken broth

1 cup chopped peeled jicama or potato

1 4-ounce can diced green chile peppers

1 teaspoon ground cumin

2 tablespoons snipped fresh cilantro

1 tablespoon lime juice

¼ cup crumbled queso fresco or feta cheese (1 ounce)

**Start to finish: 35 minutes   Makes 4 servings (5 cups)**

In a large saucepan cook onion and garlic in hot oil until tender. Stir in white kidney beans, black beans, chicken broth, jicama or potato, chile peppers, and cumin.

Bring to boiling; reduce heat. Simmer, covered, about 10 minutes or until jicama is crisp-tender or potato is tender. Stir in cilantro and lime juice; heat through. Top each serving with queso fresco or feta cheese.

Nutrition facts per serving: 254 cal., 9 g total fat (3 g sat. fat), 15 mg chol., 1,012 mg sodium, 37 g carbo., 10 g fiber, 19 g pro.  Daily values:  2% vit. A, 32% vit. C, 16% calcium, 24% iron

## the **mexican** potato

Jicama is often referred to as the Mexican potato. This large, bulbous root vegetable has a thin brown skin and white crunchy flesh. Unlike regular potatoes, jicama has a sweet, nutty flavor and is good both raw and cooked. It is available from November through May and can be purchased in Mexican markets and most large supermarkets. Jicama will last up to 5 days stored in the refrigerator. The thin skin should be peeled just before using. When cooked, jicama retains its crisp, water chestnut-type texture.

# bayou shrimp soup

Enjoy the flavor of gumbo without all the fuss. This stew incorporates familiar gumbo ingredients—rice, tomatoes, sausage, and shrimp—minus the long cooking time.

**Start to finish: 35 minutes   Makes 4 servings (6½ cups)**

In a large saucepan cook the sausage, sweet pepper, and onion over medium-high heat for 6 to 7 minutes or until vegetables are tender, stirring frequently. Add chicken broth, steak sauce, and, if using, dried thyme. If not using andouille sausage, add the crushed red pepper.

Bring to boiling; reduce heat. Simmer, covered, for 10 minutes.

Add the shrimp, tomatoes, cooked rice, and, if using, fresh thyme. Cook and stir until heated through.

Nutrition facts per serving: 404 cal., 20 g total fat (7 g sat. fat), 149 mg chol., 1,345 mg sodium, 27 g carbo., 2 g fiber, 28 g pro. Daily values: 12% vit. A, 62% vit. C, 5% calcium, 27% iron

8 ounces cooked andouille or other smoked sausage links, thinly sliced

1 medium green sweet pepper, chopped

1 medium onion, chopped

1 14½-ounce can reduced-sodium chicken broth

1 tablespoon steak sauce

2 tablespoons snipped fresh thyme or 1½ teaspoons dried thyme, crushed

¼ teaspoon crushed red pepper (optional)

8 ounces frozen, peeled, cooked shrimp

2 cups chopped tomatoes

1½ cups cooked rice

# shrimp & greens soup

Although great any time of year, this fresh-tasting seafood soup is light enough to serve during the summer. The savory combination of shrimp, shredded bok choy, and leek is embellished with an accent of lemon pepper.

**Start to finish: 30 minutes   Makes 4 servings (7 cups)**

Thaw shrimp, if frozen.

In a large saucepan cook leek and garlic in hot oil over medium-high heat about 2 minutes or until leek is tender. Carefully add chicken broth, parsley, marjoram, and lemon-pepper seasoning. Bring to boiling; add shrimp. Return to boiling; reduce heat.

Simmer, uncovered, for 2 minutes. Stir in the bok choy. Cook about 1 minute more or until the shrimp turn pink.

Nutrition facts per serving: 147 cal., 6 g total fat (1 g sat. fat), 131 mg chol., 1,093 mg sodium, 5 g carbo., 2 g fiber, 18 g pro. Daily values: 10% vit. A, 25% vit. C, 6% calcium, 18% iron

12 ounces peeled and deveined fresh or frozen shrimp

1 large leek, sliced

2 cloves garlic, minced

1 tablespoon olive oil

3 14½-ounce cans reduced-sodium chicken broth or vegetable broth

1 tablespoon snipped fresh Italian flat-leaf parsley or parsley

1 tablespoon snipped fresh marjoram or thyme

¼ teaspoon lemon-pepper seasoning

2 cups shredded bok choy or spinach leaves

# creamy chicken
## vegetable soup

Longing for a simpler way to cook? Quick-cooking rice and purchased alfredo sauce save time and effort in a soup that tastes like it took hours to prepare.

**28**

3  cups chicken broth

2  medium carrots, thinly sliced

2  stalks celery, thinly sliced

1  cup chopped cooked chicken

1  small zucchini, thinly sliced
    (about 1 cup)

½  cup uncooked quick-cooking rice

1  10-ounce container refrigerated
    light alfredo sauce

¼  cup chopped roasted red sweet
    peppers or one 4-ounce jar diced
    pimentos, drained

1  tablespoon snipped fresh thyme

**Start to finish: 30 minutes    Makes 4 servings (6 cups)**

In a Dutch oven combine chicken broth, carrots, and celery. Bring to boiling; reduce heat. Simmer, covered, for 10 minutes.

Stir in chicken, zucchini, and rice. Remove from heat and let stand, covered, about 5 minutes or until rice is tender. Stir in alfredo sauce, roasted red peppers, and thyme. Return to heat; heat through.

Nutrition facts per serving: 349 cal., 14 g total fat (7 g sat. fat), 65 mg chol., 1,286 mg sodium, 34 g carbo., 2 g fiber, 22 g pro. Daily values: 99% vit. A, 49% vit. C, 16% calcium, 12% iron

## cooked **chicken** choices

When a recipe calls for cooked chicken, you can use a package of frozen chopped cooked chicken. Or, purchase a deli-roasted chicken. A cooked whole chicken will yield 1½ to 2 cups boneless chopped meat. If you have more time, you can poach chicken breasts. For 2 cups cubed cooked chicken, in a large skillet place 12 ounces skinless, boneless chicken breasts and 1½ cups water. Bring to boiling; reduce heat. Cover and simmer for 12 to 14 minutes or until chicken is tender and no longer pink. Drain chicken well and cut up. Add to the soup and cook just long enough to heat through.

# chicken & rice soup with dumplings

This soul-warming soup will remind you of your grandmother's old-fashioned chicken and dumplings. The heat from the boiling soup helps cook the dumplings to a light, tender perfection.

**Start to finish: 35 minutes   Makes 4 or 5 servings (8 cups)**

In a large saucepan cook mushrooms, celery, and carrot in 1 tablespoon hot margarine until tender. Carefully stir in chicken broth, chicken, peas, rice, thyme, and pepper. Bring to boiling.

Meanwhile, prepare dumplings. Drop dumpling batter from a small spoon to make 16 mounds on top of the boiling soup; reduce heat. Simmer, covered, about 10 minutes or until dumplings are cooked.

**Dumplings:** In a small bowl beat together 2 eggs, $\frac{1}{4}$ cup melted margarine or butter, and $\frac{1}{4}$ teaspoon salt. Stir in $\frac{2}{3}$ cup instant flour (Wondra) or all-purpose flour.

Nutrition facts per serving: 491 cal., 28 g total fat (1 g sat. fat), 183 mg chol., 1,222 mg sodium, 37 g carbo., 3 g fiber, 33 g pro. Daily values: 83% vit. A, 11% vit. C, 5% calcium, 27% iron

1 cup sliced fresh mushrooms

1 stalk celery, sliced

1 medium carrot, chopped

1 tablespoon margarine or butter

5 cups reduced-sodium chicken broth

2 cups chopped cooked chicken

1 cup frozen peas

$\frac{1}{2}$ cup uncooked quick-cooking rice

2 teaspoons snipped fresh thyme or 1 teaspoon dried thyme, crushed

$\frac{1}{4}$ teaspoon pepper

1 recipe Dumplings

# some like it hot

# gingered pork & cabbage soup

Asian cooks have long known that the peppery, slightly sweet taste of gingerroot perfectly matches mild-flavored pork. Here, the combination is even better joined with a bit of fresh mint.

**Start to finish: 40 minutes    Makes 6 servings (10 cups)**

In a medium saucepan bring the 6 cups broth to boiling. Meanwhile, trim fat from pork. Cut pork into ½-inch cubes. In a large saucepan cook pork, onion, garlic, and gingerroot in hot oil until pork is brown.

Add vegetable broth. Bring to boiling. Stir in tomatoes and carrots. Return to boiling; reduce heat. Simmer, covered, for 15 minutes.

Stir in the pasta and cook for 6 to 8 minutes more or until pasta is tender but still firm. Stir in sliced Chinese cabbage and mint. If desired, garnish with Chinese cabbage leaves.

Nutrition facts per serving: 141 cal., 6 g total fat (1 g sat. fat), 16 mg chol., 961 mg sodium, 21 g carbo., 2 g fiber, 8 g pro. Daily values: 65% vit. A, 47% vit. C, 5% calcium, 14% iron

| | |
|---|---|
| 6 | cups vegetable broth or chicken broth |
| 8 | ounces boneless pork sirloin, cut ½ inch thick |
| 1 | large onion, chopped |
| 4 | cloves garlic, minced |
| 2 | teaspoons grated gingerroot |
| 1 | tablespoon cooking oil |
| 3 | small tomatoes, chopped |
| 2 | medium carrots, finely chopped |
| ½ | cup dried anelli pasta |
| 4 | cups thinly sliced Chinese cabbage |
| ¼ | cup snipped fresh mint |
| | Chinese cabbage leaves (optional) |

## vegetable broth business

When a recipe calls for vegetable broth, you can use canned broth or bouillon cubes, or prepare a homemade stock. An easy way to make your own vegetable stock is to save the water in which vegetables are boiled and freeze it in a covered container. Keep saving the liquid from the vegetables you prepare, and in the course of time you will have a basic vegetable stock that's ready to use.

# chinese glass noodle soup

Tender strips of pork, broccoli, and bean threads comprise the main ingredients in this broth-based soup. Crushed red pepper, gingerroot, and toasted sesame oil supply the prominent Asian flavor.

2 ounces bean threads
   (cellophane noodles)

2 cloves garlic, minced

1 tablespoon grated gingerroot

2 tablespoons cooking oil

3 cups broccoli flowerets

12 ounces lean boneless pork,
   cut into bite-size strips

3 14½-ounce cans reduced-sodium
   chicken broth

1 teaspoon crushed red pepper

1 teaspoon toasted sesame oil

**Start to finish: 30 minutes   Makes 4 servings (8 cups)**

Place bean threads in a bowl; pour enough boiling water over bean threads to cover. Let stand for 10 minutes; drain. Use scissors to cut bean threads into 2-inch lengths; set aside.

Meanwhile, in a large saucepan cook the garlic and gingerroot in 1 tablespoon hot cooking oil over medium heat for 15 seconds. Add the broccoli. Cover and cook for 3 to 4 minutes or until crisp-tender, stirring once or twice. Remove mixture from saucepan; set aside.

Add remaining cooking oil to saucepan. Add the pork; cook and stir for 2 to 3 minutes or until slightly pink in center. Carefully add chicken broth, red pepper, and sesame oil. Bring to boiling; reduce heat. Stir in bean threads and vegetable mixture; heat through.

Nutrition facts per serving: 283 cal., 15 g total fat (3 g sat. fat), 38 mg chol., 989 mg sodium, 18 g carbo., 2 g fiber, 18 g pro. Daily values: 7% vit. A, 54% vit. C, 2% calcium, 7% iron

# garlic, black bean, & sausage soup

Cuban flavors dominate this black bean soup, which features a hearty combination of sausage, tomatoes, and fennel seed. A spoonful of sour cream tops each serving.

**Start to finish: 40 minutes   Makes 4 or 5 servings (6 cups)**

In a large saucepan cook sausage, onion, garlic, and fennel seed over medium-high heat for 10 to 12 minutes or until sausage is no longer pink. Drain well.

Stir in the black beans and beef broth. Bring to boiling; reduce heat. Simmer, covered, for 15 minutes.

Meanwhile, if desired, stir the red pepper into the sour cream. Cover and refrigerate until ready to serve.

Just before serving, stir the tomatoes and oregano into soup; heat through.* Top each serving with sour cream mixture.

Nutrition facts per serving: 429 cal., 20 g total fat (8 g sat. fat), 55 mg chol., 1,453 mg sodium, 42 g carbo., 12 g fiber, 30 g pro. Daily values: 10% vit. A, 44% vit. C, 11% calcium, 27% iron

*Note: If a thinner consistency is desired, add a small amount of water.*

12 ounces bulk mild Italian sausage

1½ cups chopped onion

10 cloves garlic, minced

½ teaspoon fennel seed, crushed

2 15-ounce cans black beans, drained and rinsed

1 14½-ounce can beef broth

Dash ground red pepper (optional)

¼ cup dairy sour cream

2 cups chopped tomatoes

2 tablespoons snipped fresh oregano

# caribbean-style pork stew

The flavor of a plantain will depend on the ripeness. A ripe, black-skinned plantain tastes like a banana. An almost-ripe, yellow plantain tastes similar to sweet potatoes. Unripe, green plantains taste starchy but lose the starchy flavor upon cooking.

34

1 15-ounce can black beans, drained and rinsed

1 14½-ounce can beef broth

1¾ cups water

12 ounces cooked lean boneless pork, cut into bite-size strips

3 plantains, peeled and cubed

1 cup chopped tomatoes

½ of a 16-ounce package (2 cups) frozen pepper stir-fry vegetables (such as yellow, green, and red sweet peppers and onion)

1 tablespoon grated gingerroot

1 teaspoon ground cumin

¼ teaspoon crushed red pepper

¼ teaspoon salt

3 cups hot cooked rice

Crushed red pepper (optional)

Fresh pineapple slices (optional)

**Start to finish: 30 minutes  Makes 6 servings (8½ cups)**

In a Dutch oven combine the beans, broth, and water; heat to boiling.

Add the pork, plantains, and tomatoes to the bean mixture. Stir in the frozen vegetables, gingerroot, cumin, the ¼ teaspoon red pepper, and the salt. Return mixture to boiling; reduce heat and simmer, covered, for 10 minutes or until plantains are tender. Serve with hot rice. If desired, sprinkle with additional crushed red pepper and garnish with pineapple.

Nutrition facts per serving: 425 cal., 9 g total fat (3 g sat. fat), 52 mg chol., 547 mg sodium, 66 carbo., 6 g fiber, 26 g pro. Daily values: 44% vit. A, 62% vit. C, 5% calcium, 4% iron

# yucatan soup with lime

The bright flavors of the Yucatan dance in your mouth as you sip this highly spiced soup. The addition of lime juice provides a tangy surprise.

12 ounces skinless, boneless chicken breasts, cut into bite-size pieces

3 cloves garlic, minced

1 tablespoon olive oil or cooking oil

1 tablespoon hot chili powder

½ teaspoon cumin seed, crushed, or ¼ teaspoon ground cumin

¼ to ½ teaspoon crushed red pepper (optional)

2 14½-ounce cans chicken broth

½ cup chopped green onions

1 large tomato, chopped

3 tablespoons lime juice

**Start to finish: 30 minutes   Makes 4 servings (5½ cups)**

In a Dutch oven cook the chicken and garlic in hot oil over medium-high heat until chicken is no longer pink. Stir in chili powder, cumin, and, if desired, crushed red pepper. Cook and stir for 30 seconds. Stir in the chicken broth and green onions.

Bring to boiling; reduce heat. Simmer, uncovered, for 10 minutes. Remove from heat. Stir in the tomato and lime juice.

Nutrition facts per serving: 178 cal., 8 g total fat (1 g sat. fat), 45 mg chol., 719 mg sodium, 6 g carbo., 1 g fiber, 21 g pro. Daily values: 12% vit. A, 25% vit. C, 2% calcium, 12% iron

# pork, corn, &
## three-pepper soup

Experience a peck of peppers in this soup. There are actually three different types of peppers in this corn-filled soup: red sweet pepper, green chile peppers, and hot ground red pepper. Adjust the heat level by adding more or less ground red pepper.

**Start to finish: 30 minutes   Makes 4 servings (5½ cups)**

In a large saucepan cook pork in hot oil for 2 to 3 minutes or until slightly pink in center. Remove from pan; cover and keep warm. Add red sweet pepper and onion to saucepan and cook until tender.

Stir in the cream-style corn, chicken broth, milk, frozen corn, and undrained chile peppers. Bring to boiling; reduce heat. Simmer, covered, for 5 minutes.

Stir in pork, parsley, salt, and ground red pepper; heat through.

Nutrition facts per serving: 281 cal., 12 g total fat (3 g sat. fat), 43 mg chol., 768 mg sodium, 30 g carbo., 2 g fiber, 19 g pro. Daily values: 18% vit. A, 73% vit. C, 10% calcium, 10% iron

12  ounces lean boneless pork,
      cut into bite-size strips

 1  tablespoon cooking oil

 ½  cup chopped red sweet pepper

 1  small onion, chopped

 1  14¾-ounce can cream-style corn

 1  cup chicken broth

 1  cup milk

 ½  cup frozen whole kernel corn

 1  4-ounce can diced green
      chile peppers

 ¼  cup snipped fresh parsley

 ¼  teaspoon salt

 ¼  teaspoon ground red pepper

# chicken chili with rice

Tomatillos often are referred to as Mexican green tomatoes because they resemble a small green tomato and are often used in Mexican cooking. They hint of a lemon and apple flavor. Tomatillos add a unique taste to salads, salsas, and this chunky soup.

**Start to finish: 35 minutes   Makes 4 servings (5 cups)**

In a large saucepan cook the garlic and jalapeño pepper in hot oil for 30 seconds. Carefully stir in onions, chicken broth, chili powder, cumin, oregano, salt, white pepper, and red pepper.

Bring to boiling; reduce heat. Simmer, covered, for 20 minutes. Add beans, chicken, and tomatillos; cook and stir until heated through. Serve over rice.

Nutrition facts per serving: 335 cal., 8 g total fat (1 g sat. fat), 34 mg chol., 417 mg sodium, 51 g carbo., 8 g fiber, 23 g pro. Daily values: 6% vit. A, 23% vit. C, 6% calcium, 26% iron

3 cloves garlic, minced

1 fresh jalapeño pepper, seeded and finely chopped

1 tablespoon cooking oil

2 cups frozen small whole onions

1 cup reduced-sodium chicken broth or chicken broth

2 teaspoons chili powder

1 teaspoon ground cumin

1 teaspoon dried oregano, crushed

¼ teaspoon salt

⅛ teaspoon ground white pepper

⅛ teaspoon ground red pepper

1 19-ounce can white kidney (cannellini) beans, drained and rinsed

1 cup chopped cooked chicken

1 cup chopped tomatillos

2 cups hot cooked rice or couscous

# chipotle chile pepper soup

If you have never tried chipotle (chih-POHT-lay) peppers, jalapeño peppers that have been smoked, here's your chance. As well as adding the heat, these peppers add a pleasant smoked flavor.

1 large onion, finely chopped

4 cloves garlic, minced

1 tablespoon olive oil or cooking oil

12 ounces skinless, boneless chicken breasts, cut into bite-size pieces

1 14½-ounce can chicken broth

2 teaspoons chopped canned chipotle peppers in adobo sauce

½ teaspoon sugar

¼ teaspoon salt

2 cups chopped tomatoes or one 14½-ounce can low-sodium diced tomatoes

¼ cup snipped fresh cilantro

**Start to finish: 35 minutes   Makes 3 servings (4 cups)**

In a Dutch oven cook the onion and garlic in hot oil over medium-high heat about 4 minutes or until tender. Add the chicken; cook for 2 minutes. Stir in the chicken broth, chipotle peppers, sugar, and salt.

Bring to boiling; reduce heat. Simmer, uncovered, for 15 minutes. Remove from heat. Stir in the tomatoes and the snipped cilantro.

Nutrition facts per serving: 246 cal., 9 g total fat (2 g sat. fat), 60 mg chol., 735 mg sodium, 14 g carbo., 3 g fiber, 26 g pro. Daily values: 16% vit. A, 53% vit. C, 3% calcium, 13% iron

*Note: The sugar cuts the sharpness of the tomatoes, giving a mellow, rich flavor to the soup without adding noticeable sweetness.*

## finishing **touches**
Keep the soup garnishes simple. A sprinkling of snipped fresh herbs or sliced green onions adds nice color to any soup, while croutons offer a little crunch. A slice of lemon, a little grated cheese, a few chopped nuts, sieved cooked egg white or yolk, or shredded radishes add complementary color to many soups.

# mushroom tortelloni in curry cream

Indonesian in flavor, this quick-cooking soup captures your attention with its wonderful aroma. Curry, coconut, and basil all add to the allure. If you're unable to find tortelloni, a larger version of tortellini, use tortellini instead.

42

1  **shallot, finely chopped**

1  **fresh jalapeño pepper, seeded and finely chopped**

1  **clove garlic, minced**

2  **teaspoons curry powder**

1  **tablespoon cooking oil**

1  **14½-ounce can chicken broth**

1  **14-ounce can unsweetened coconut milk**

1  **9-ounce package refrigerated mushroom tortelloni**

1  **tablespoon snipped fresh basil**

1  **medium tomato, chopped**

   **Chopped peanuts (optional)**

**Start to finish: 30 minutes   Makes 4 servings (5 cups)**

In a medium saucepan cook shallot, jalapeño pepper, garlic, and curry powder in hot oil about 1 minute or until shallot is tender. Stir in chicken broth. Bring to boiling; reduce heat. Simmer, covered, for 5 minutes.

Stir in the coconut milk, tortelloni, and basil. Cook and stir about 5 minutes more or until pasta is tender but still firm. Stir in the tomato. Cook and stir until heated through, but do not boil.

If desired, garnish each serving with peanuts.

Nutrition facts per serving: 306 cal., 14 g total fat (7 g sat. fat), 24 mg chol., 649 mg sodium, 35 g carbo., 3 g fiber, 10 g pro. Daily values: 8% vit. A, 20% vit. C, 9% calcium, 18% iron

# thai red curry soup with shrimp

Red curry paste, an essential ingredient in Thai cooking, imparts spiciness to this soup. Coconut milk, often called for in curry dishes, can be purchased in cans at Asian markets and some supermarkets.

44

1 tablespoon cooking oil

12 ounces peeled and deveined fresh shrimp, halved lengthwise

1 tablespoon red curry paste

1 14½-ounce can chicken broth

1 tablespoon fish sauce (optional)

8 ounces green beans, trimmed and cut into bite-size pieces, or one 9-ounce package frozen cut green beans, thawed

1 cup unsweetened coconut milk

2 tablespoons snipped fresh basil

**Start to finish: 25 minutes   Makes 4 servings (5 cups)**

Pour cooking oil into a large saucepan; preheat over medium-high heat. Stir-fry shrimp and curry paste in hot oil for 2 to 3 minutes or until shrimp turn pink. Remove shrimp from saucepan; set aside.

In same saucepan bring the chicken broth and, if desired, fish sauce to boiling. Add the green beans. Return to boiling; reduce heat.

Simmer, uncovered, about 5 minutes or until beans are crisp-tender. Stir in shrimp and coconut milk; heat through. Stir in basil.

Nutrition facts per serving: 249 cal., 16 g total fat (11 g sat. fat), 131 mg chol., 656 mg sodium, 8 g carbo., 2 g fiber, 19 g pro. Daily values: 9% vit. A, 11% vit. C, 5% calcium, 24% iron

## selecting **shrimp**

Shrimp are sold by the pound. The price per pound usually is determined by the size of the shrimp—the bigger the shrimp, the higher the price and the fewer per pound. Fresh shrimp should be moist and firm, have translucent flesh, and smell fresh. Signs of poor quality are an ammonia smell and blackened edges or spots on the shells.

# cajun fish soup

This tongue-tingling soup gets its spirited flavor from Cajun seasoning, a blend of ingredients such as garlic, chiles, black pepper, and mustard. Depending on the brand of seasoning you buy, however, the combination of ingredients may vary.

**Start to finish: 25 minutes   Makes 4 servings (7½ cups)**

Thaw the fish or shrimp, if frozen. If using fish, cut into 1-inch pieces; set fish aside.

In a large saucepan or Dutch oven combine the vegetable or chicken broth, mushrooms, summer squash or zucchini, onion, garlic, and Cajun seasoning. Bring to boiling; reduce heat. Simmer, covered, for 5 minutes or until the vegetables are tender.

Stir in the fish or shrimp and undrained tomatoes. Bring just to boiling; reduce heat. Simmer, covered, for 2 to 3 minutes or until the fish flakes easily with a fork or the shrimp turn pink. Remove from heat. Stir in the oregano and lemon peel.

Nutrition facts per serving: 149 cal., 2 gm total fat (0 gm sat. fat), 40 mg chol., 608 mg sodium, 20 gm carbo., 5 gm fiber, 17 gm pro. Daily values: 18% vit. A, 32% vit. C, 4% calcium, 9% iron

- 12  ounces fresh or frozen fish fillets or peeled and deveined shrimp
- 1  14½-ounce can vegetable broth or chicken broth
- 1  cup sliced fresh mushrooms
- 1  small yellow summer squash or zucchini, halved lengthwise and sliced
- ½  cup chopped onion
- 1  clove garlic, minced
- 1  to 1½ teaspoons Cajun seasoning
- 2  14½-ounce cans reduced-sodium stewed tomatoes
- 2  tablespoons snipped fresh oregano
- ½  teaspoon finely shredded lemon peel

everyday
gourmet

# asian chicken noodle soup

Chicken soup is known universally as a comforting cure-all for the body and soul. Soy sauce, gingerroot, and pea pods add an Asian flair to this version of a classic favorite.

**Start to finish: 20 minutes   Makes 3 servings (5½ cups)**

In a large saucepan combine chicken broth, water, noodles, soy sauce, gingerroot, and crushed red pepper. Bring to boiling. Stir in the sweet pepper, carrot, and green onions. Return to boiling; reduce heat. Simmer, covered, for 4 to 6 minutes or until vegetables are crisp-tender and noodles are tender.

Stir in chicken and pea pods. Simmer, uncovered, for 1 to 2 minutes more or until pea pods are crisp-tender.

Nutrition facts per serving: 224 cal., 6 g total fat (2 g sat. fat), 58 mg chol., 1,280 mg sodium, 17 g carbo., 2 g fiber, 24 g pro. Daily values: 76% vit. A, 82% vit. C, 4% calcium, 19% iron

2 14½-ounce cans chicken broth

1 cup water

¾ cup dried fine egg noodles

1 tablespoon soy sauce

1 teaspoon grated gingerroot

⅛ teaspoon crushed red pepper

1 medium red sweet pepper, cut into ¾-inch pieces

1 medium carrot, chopped

⅓ cup thinly sliced green onions

1 cup chopped cooked chicken or turkey

1 cup fresh pea pods, halved crosswise, or ½ of a 6-ounce package frozen pea pods, thawed and halved crosswise

# fish provençale

The sweet essence of fresh fennel blends nicely with fish, tomatoes, garlic, and onion. This orange-scented soup tastes as good as it smells.

48

8 ounces fresh or frozen skinless haddock, grouper, or halibut fillets

1 small fennel bulb

3 cups vegetable broth or chicken broth

1 large onion, finely chopped

1 small yellow summer squash, cubed (about 1 cup)

1 cup dry white wine

1 teaspoon finely shredded orange or lemon peel

3 cloves garlic, minced

2 cups chopped tomatoes or one 14½-ounce can diced tomatoes

2 tablespoons snipped fresh thyme

**Start to finish: 30 minutes   Makes 4 servings (8 cups)**

Thaw fish, if frozen. Cut fish into 1-inch pieces; set aside.

Cut off and discard upper stalks of fennel. Remove any wilted outer layers; cut a thin slice from base. Wash fennel; cut in half lengthwise and thinly slice.

In a large saucepan combine fennel, vegetable broth, onion, squash, wine, orange peel, and garlic. Bring to boiling; reduce heat. Simmer, covered, for 10 minutes. Stir in fish pieces, tomatoes, and thyme. Cook about 3 minutes more or just until fish flakes easily. If desired, garnish with additional snipped thyme.

Nutrition facts per serving: 156 cal., 3 g total fat (0 g sat. fat), 18 mg chol., 752 mg sodium, 15 g carbo., 8 g fiber, 14 g pro. Daily values: 11% vit. A, 46% vit. C, 6% calcium, 16% iron

## soup with spirit

Adding wine to soup often enhances its flavor. Sherry or Madeira blends well with veal or chicken soup. A strongly flavored soup with beef benefits from a tablespoon of dry red table wine. And dry white table wine adds zest to fish soup, crab or lobster bisque, or creamy chowder. Be thrifty with salt in a soup to which wine is added, as the wine intensifies saltiness.

# paella soup

Brighten the menu when you serve this colorful soup. From the root of a tropical plant, turmeric gives this rice, shrimp, and pork mixture an inviting yellow glow. Once applied as a perfume many years ago, turmeric is now used to flavor foods.

**Start to finish: 35 minutes   Makes 4 servings (6½ cups)**

In a large saucepan cook green onions, sweet pepper, and garlic in hot oil 2 minutes.

Stir in chicken broth, rice, bay leaf, salt, red pepper, and turmeric. Heat to boiling; reduce heat. Simmer, covered, for 15 minutes. Stir in the cooked pork, shrimp, and peas. Simmer, covered, for 3 to 5 minutes more or until shrimp turn pink. Remove bay leaf. Stir in fresh oregano.

Nutrition facts per serving: 324 cal., 10 g total fat (3 g sat. fat), 139 mg chol., 879 mg sodium, 25 g carbo., 2 g fiber, 31 g pro. Daily values: 13% vit. A, 29% vit. C, 3% calcium, 25% iron

- ½ cup thinly sliced green onions
- ⅓ cup chopped red sweet pepper
- 1 clove garlic, minced
- 1 teaspoon cooking oil
- 1 14½-ounce can reduced-sodium chicken broth
- ½ cup uncooked long grain rice
- 1 bay leaf
- ¼ teaspoon salt
- ⅛ teaspoon ground red pepper
- ⅛ teaspoon ground turmeric
- 8 ounces cooked pork, cut into ¾-inch cubes
- 8 ounces peeled and deveined fresh shrimp
- 1 cup frozen peas
- 2 teaspoons snipped fresh oregano

# sherried smoked salmon soup

Lox-style salmon is the star ingredient in this cream soup. Stir in the flaked, paper-thin strips of brine-cured pink salmon and a touch of sherry and dill just before serving.

52

3 cups sliced fresh shiitake
   or other mushrooms

¾ cup thinly sliced leeks or ½ cup
   thinly sliced green onions

1 tablespoon margarine or butter

2 cups chicken broth or
   vegetable broth

2 cups milk

2 tablespoons cornstarch

4 ounces thinly sliced smoked
   salmon (lox-style), flaked

2 tablespoons dry sherry

1 tablespoon snipped fresh dill

**Start to finish: 30 minutes   Makes 4 servings (5 cups)**

In a large saucepan cook mushrooms and leeks in hot margarine until tender. Stir in chicken broth. Bring to boiling.

Meanwhile, combine milk and cornstarch; stir into mushroom mixture. Cook and stir over medium heat until thickened and bubbly. Cook and stir for 2 minutes more. Stir in salmon, sherry, and dill; heat through.

Nutrition facts per serving: 262 cal., 8 g total fat (3 g sat. fat), 16 mg chol., 722 mg sodium, 35 g carbo., 4 g fiber, 14 g pro. Daily values: 12% vit. A, 14% vit. C, 16% calcium, 15% iron

### smoked salmon

Smoked salmon is fresh salmon that has been smoked by either hot- or cold-smoking methods. Lox is brine-cured cold-smoked, which often makes the salmon taste a bit saltier than other smoking methods. Some lox may have a little sugar added to the brine, making it less salty. Look for lox in the seafood section of the supermarket or specialty food shops. Because it is smoked, it is ready to eat.

# spicy caramelized onion soup

A spoonful of sugar really does make these onions cook down in the most delightful way. In addition, the melted sugar adds a rich caramel flavor to the white wine and chicken broth in this flavorful soup.

**Start to finish: 30 minutes   Makes 4 servings (5 cups)**

In a medium saucepan cook onions and Cajun seasoning in hot oil until onions are tender, stirring frequently. Sprinkle with brown sugar; cook for 1 to 2 minutes more or until onions are golden. Stir in flour; cook for 1 minute more.

Stir in chicken broth, chicken, wine, and pepper; cook and stir until heated through. Top each serving with blue cheese and parsley.

Nutrition facts per serving: 302 cal., 18 g total fat (5 g sat. fat), 48 mg chol., 1,334 mg sodium, 14 g carbo., 1 g fiber, 18 g pro. Daily values: 6% vit. A, 7% vit. C, 6% calcium, 12% iron

3 medium onions, thinly sliced (about 2¼ cups)

2 teaspoons Cajun seasoning

2 tablespoons cooking oil

1 tablespoon brown sugar

1 tablespoon all-purpose flour

4 cups chicken broth

1½ cups chopped cooked smoked chicken

¼ cup dry white wine

⅛ teaspoon pepper

¼ cup crumbled blue cheese or shredded Gruyère cheese (1 ounce)

1 tablespoon snipped fresh parsley

# chicken & shrimp
## tortilla soup

Your family will be intrigued when you sprinkle shreds of crisp-baked corn tortillas over the top of this eye-catching Southwestern soup. Make the tortilla shreds ahead of time and store them in an airtight container.

54

6 ounces peeled and deveined fresh or frozen medium shrimp

1 recipe Crisp Tortilla Shreds

1 large onion, chopped

1 teaspoon cumin seed

1 tablespoon cooking oil

4½ cups reduced-sodium chicken broth

1 14½-ounce can Mexican-style stewed tomatoes

3 tablespoons snipped fresh cilantro

2 tablespoons lime juice

1⅔ cups shredded cooked chicken breast

**Start to finish: 30 minutes   Makes 6 servings (7¾ cups)**

Thaw shrimp, if frozen. Prepare Crisp Tortilla Shreds; set aside.

In a large saucepan cook the onion and cumin seed in hot oil about 5 minutes or until onion is tender. Carefully add chicken broth, undrained tomatoes, cilantro, and lime juice.

Bring to boiling; reduce heat. Simmer, covered, for 8 minutes. Stir in shrimp and chicken. Cook about 3 minutes more or until shrimp turn pink, stirring occasionally. Top each serving with tortilla shreds.

**Crisp Tortilla Shreds:** Brush four 5½-inch corn tortillas with 1 tablespoon cooking oil. In a small bowl combine ½ teaspoon salt and ⅛ teaspoon pepper; sprinkle mixture over tortillas. Cut tortillas into thin shreds. Arrange in a single layer on a baking sheet. Bake in a 350° oven about 8 minutes or until crisp.

Nutrition facts per serving: 160 cal., 5 g total fat (1 g sat. fat), 80 mg chol., 794 mg sodium, 8 g carbo., 0 g fiber, 21 g pro. Daily values: 7% vit. A, 22% vit. C, 2% calcium, 10% iron

# hot & sour turkey soup

The Chinese and Mediterranean technique of cooking egg drops in soup is featured here. The egg cooks in thin, swirling threads as it is stirred slowly into the hot soup.

3½  cups chicken broth

2  cups sliced fresh mushrooms

3  tablespoons rice vinegar
    or white vinegar

2  tablespoons soy sauce or
    reduced-sodium soy sauce

1  teaspoon sugar

1  teaspoon grated gingerroot

¼  to ½ teaspoon pepper

1  tablespoon cornstarch

1  tablespoon cold water

2  cups shredded cooked turkey

2  cups sliced bok choy

1  6-ounce package frozen pea pods

1  beaten egg

3  tablespoons thinly sliced
    green onions

**Start to finish: 30 minutes   Makes 4 servings (6⅔ cups)**

In a large saucepan combine chicken broth, mushrooms, vinegar, soy sauce, sugar, gingerroot, and pepper. Bring to boiling.

Meanwhile, stir together cornstarch and cold water; stir into broth mixture. Cook and stir until thickened and bubbly. Cook and stir for 2 minutes more. Stir in turkey, bok choy, and pea pods.

Pour the egg into the soup in a steady stream while stirring 2 or 3 times to create shreds. Remove from heat. Stir in green onions.

Nutrition facts per serving: 238 cal., 6 g total fat (2 g sat. fat), 108 mg chol., 1,275 mg sodium, 15 g carbo., 4 g fiber, 30 g pro. Daily values: 4% vit. A, 49% vit. C, 7% calcium, 27% iron

## the **facts** on **rice vinegar**

Rice vinegar, made from rice wine or sake, has a subtle tang and slightly sweet taste. Chinese rice vinegars are stronger than Japanese vinegars, although both are slightly milder than most vinegars. Chinese rice vinegar comes in three types: white (clear or pale yellow), used mainly in hot-and-sour or sweet-and-sour dishes; red, a typical accompaniment for boiled or steamed shellfish; and black, used mainly as a condiment.

# mushroom-noodle
## & tofu soup

Japanese udon (oo-DOHN) noodles are similar to spaghetti. Look for them in Asian markets or in the Oriental section of your supermarket.

**Start to finish: 30 minutes   Makes 6 servings (9 cups)**

In a large saucepan bring the broth to boiling. Meanwhile, in a medium mixing bowl gently stir together tofu cubes, soy sauce, and sesame oil; set aside.

In a medium saucepan cook the sliced mushrooms, gingerroot, and garlic in hot cooking oil for 4 minutes. Add to the hot broth. Stir in the frozen vegetables and udon noodles. Bring to boiling; reduce heat.

Simmer, covered, for 10 to 12 minutes or until vegetables and noodles are tender, stirring once or twice. Gently stir in the tofu mixture and the cilantro; heat through.

Nutrition facts per serving: 162 cal., 7 g total fat (1 g sat. fat), 0 mg chol., 868 mg sodium, 17 g carbo., 1 g fiber, 9 g pro. Daily values: 46% vit. A, 35% vit. C, 3% calcium, 9% iron

1  **49-ounce can reduced-sodium chicken broth (about 6 cups)**

1  **10- to 12-ounce package extra-firm tofu (fresh bean curd), drained and cut into ½-inch cubes**

1  **tablespoon soy sauce**

1  **tablespoon toasted sesame oil**

6  **ounces sliced fresh shiitake or button mushrooms (about 2¼ cups)**

1  **tablespoon grated gingerroot**

1  **clove garlic, minced**

1  **tablespoon cooking oil**

1  **16-ounce package frozen sugar snap stir-fry vegetables**

2  **ounces dried udon noodles or spaghetti, broken**

1  **tablespoon snipped fresh cilantro**

# brandied mushroom soup with herbs

Mushroom lovers will ask for this brandy-and-thyme-seasoned soup time and again. It's a satisfying meal when served over slices of toasted French bread. Just add a tossed green salad and a robust red wine.

3   cups sliced fresh mushrooms

1   medium onion, finely chopped

1   tablespoon olive oil

¼   cup all-purpose flour

2   14½-ounce cans beef broth

2   tablespoons brandy or dry white wine (optional)

1½  teaspoons snipped fresh thyme or ½ teaspoon dried thyme, crushed

1   teaspoon Worcestershire sauce

2   tablespoons snipped fresh parsley

4   slices toasted French bread (optional)

**Start to finish: 30 minutes   Makes 3 servings (4½ cups)**

In a large saucepan cook the mushrooms and onion in hot oil until onion is tender. Stir in flour; gradually stir in beef broth, brandy (if desired), dried thyme (if using), and Worcestershire sauce.

Cook and stir until slightly thickened and bubbly. Cook and stir for 1 minute more. Stir in the parsley and, if using, fresh thyme. If desired, serve over slices of French bread.

Nutrition facts per serving: 125 cal., 6 g total fat (1 g sat. fat), 0 mg chol., 913 mg sodium, 14 g carbo., 2 g fiber, 6 g pro. Daily values: 1% vit. A, 16% vit. C, 3% calcium, 17% iron

## marvelous mushrooms

There are so many types of mushrooms available at your supermarket. Try experimenting with different varieties. It is usually easy to find the common white or brown mushroom, often referred to as button mushrooms. They are usually very mild in flavor. For a richer, earthier flavor try morels, shiitakes, or portobellos. The best way to clean mushrooms is to brush them off with a clean, soft vegetable brush and wipe them with a clean, damp cloth. Do not soak mushrooms because they're like a sponge and the water will ruin their firm texture.

# middle eastern
## sausage & beans

Fragrant spices, such as cinnamon and allspice, often flavor Middle Eastern dishes. In this dish, raisins enhance the spices and sausage, adding a delicate, sweet taste. If you like, hot pepper sauce adds heat.

**Start to finish: 35 minutes   Makes 4 servings (5½ cups)**

In a Dutch oven cook sausage and onion until sausage is no longer pink. Drain well. Stir in cinnamon and allspice; cook for 1 minute.

Stir in the water, kidney beans, and raisins. Bring to boiling; reduce heat. Simmer, covered, for 15 minutes.

Stir in the tomatoes; heat through. If desired, serve with hot pepper sauce.

Nutrition facts per serving: 365 cal., 17 g total fat (6 g sat. fat), 49 mg chol., 764 mg sodium, 38 g carbo., 8 g fiber, 22 g pro. Daily values: 6% vit. A, 41% vit. C, 6% calcium, 21% iron

*Note: This also is delicious served over hot cooked rice tossed with toasted pecans.*

12 ounces bulk hot or mild
    Italian sausage

1½ cups chopped onion

 1 teaspoon ground cinnamon

¼ teaspoon ground allspice

 2 cups water

 1 15-ounce can dark red kidney
    beans, rinsed and drained

⅓ cup raisins

 2 cups chopped tomatoes

    Bottled hot pepper sauce (optional)

# garden varieties

# fennel-asparagus soup

Savor the splendor of spring in this garden-fresh soup. Small onions, baby carrots, and tender asparagus partner with baby lima beans for a bowlful of bounty.

61

**Start to finish: 40 minutes   Makes 4 servings (8 cups)**

In a Dutch oven combine the chicken broth, lima beans, onions, fennel seed, and pepper. Bring to boiling; reduce heat. Simmer, covered, for 10 minutes. Stir in the carrots and cook for 5 minutes.

Meanwhile, cut off and discard upper stalks of fennel, reserving leaves. Snip ¼ cup fennel leaves; set aside. Remove any wilted outer layers from bulb; cut a thin slice from base. Wash and chop fennel.

Stir the chopped fennel, asparagus, and pancetta into Dutch oven. Cook about 5 minutes more or until vegetables are tender. Garnish each serving with the reserved fennel leaves.

Nutrition facts per serving: 269 cal., 7 g total fat (2 g sat. fat), 8 mg chol., 1,329 mg sodium, 34 g carbo., 15 g fiber, 20 g pro. Daily values: 85% vit. A, 38% vit. C, 7% calcium, 26% iron

6 cups chicken broth

1 10-ounce package frozen baby lima beans

1 cup small red boiling onions, whole pearl onions, or coarsely chopped onion

1 teaspoon fennel seed, crushed

¼ teaspoon pepper

1 cup packaged, peeled baby carrots

1 medium fennel bulb

12 ounces asparagus spears, trimmed and cut into 1-inch pieces

4 ounces pancetta, chopped, crisp-cooked, and drained, or 5 slices bacon, crisp-cooked, drained, and crumbled

# turkey & mushroom soup

Orzo pasta thickens this soup of fresh mushrooms and turkey. In Italian, the word "orzo" means barley, but it's actually a tiny pasta shaped like grains of rice.

2 cups sliced fresh mushrooms (such as crimini, shiitake, porcini, or button)

1 stalk celery, thinly sliced

1 medium carrot, thinly sliced

1 small onion, chopped

1 tablespoon margarine or butter

4½ cups water

1 tablespoon instant beef bouillon granules

⅛ teaspoon pepper

½ cup dried orzo pasta (rosamarina)

1½ cups chopped cooked turkey

2 tablespoons snipped fresh parsley

1 teaspoon snipped fresh thyme

**Start to finish: 35 minutes   Makes 4 servings (6 cups)**

In a large saucepan cook mushrooms, celery, carrot, and onion in hot margarine until crisp-tender. Add water, bouillon granules, and pepper.

Bring to boiling; stir in orzo. Return to boiling; reduce heat. Simmer, uncovered, for 5 to 8 minutes or until orzo is tender but still firm. Stir in turkey, parsley, and thyme; heat through.

Nutrition facts per serving: 199 cal., 6 g total fat (2 g sat. fat), 40 mg chol., 767 mg sodium, 17 g carbo, 2 g fiber, 19 g pro. Daily values: 63% vit. A, 10% vit. C, 4% calcium, 17% iron

# caraway cabbage-sausage soup

Here, the nutty, delicate anise flavor of caraway seed is matched with cabbage, apples, and turkey kielbasa. This hearty soup is just what you'll want on a cold winter night.

**Start to finish: 30 minutes  Makes 4 servings (7 cups)**

In a large saucepan cook cabbage mix, onion, celery, and caraway seed in hot margarine or butter until vegetables are crisp-tender.

Stir in chicken broth, turkey kielbasa, apples, and pepper. Bring to boiling; reduce heat. Simmer, covered, for 5 minutes.

Nutrition facts per serving: 292 cal., 14 g total fat (3 g sat. fat), 57 mg chol., 1,486 mg sodium, 29 g carbo., 6 g fiber, 19 g pro. Daily values: 47% vit. A, 52% vit. C, 6% calcium, 15% iron

| | |
|---|---|
| 3 | cups packaged shredded cabbage with carrot (coleslaw mix) |
| 1 | medium onion, chopped |
| 1 | stalk celery, chopped |
| 1½ | teaspoons caraway seed |
| 2 | tablespoons margarine or butter |
| 4 | cups reduced-sodium chicken broth |
| 12 | ounces cooked turkey kielbasa, halved lengthwise and sliced |
| 2 | medium apples, cored and chopped |
| ¼ | teaspoon pepper |

# chicken stew with tortellini

Dress up leftover chicken by stirring it into this easy-to-prepare stew. Chunks of yellow squash and sweet pepper accompany plump tortellini and beet greens.

2  **cups water**

1  **14½-ounce can reduced-sodium chicken broth**

1  **medium yellow summer squash**

6  **cups torn beet greens, turnip greens, or spinach**

1  **green sweet pepper, coarsely chopped**

1  **cup dried cheese-filled tortellini pasta**

1  **medium onion, cut into thin wedges**

1  **medium carrot, sliced**

1½  **teaspoons snipped fresh rosemary**

½  **teaspoon salt-free seasoning blend**

¼  **teaspoon pepper**

2  **cups chopped cooked chicken**

1  **tablespoon snipped fresh basil**

**Start to finish: 35 minutes   Makes 6 servings (7½ cups)**

In a Dutch oven bring water and chicken broth to boiling. Meanwhile, halve summer squash lengthwise and cut into ½-inch slices. Add squash, greens, sweet pepper, pasta, onion, carrot, rosemary, seasoning blend, and pepper to Dutch oven.

Return to boiling; reduce heat. Simmer, covered, about 15 minutes or until pasta and vegetables are nearly tender.

Stir in chicken. Cook, covered, about 5 minutes more or until pasta and vegetables are tender. Stir fresh basil into soup.

Nutrition facts per serving: 234 cal., 6 g total fat (1 g sat. fat), 45 mg chol., 530 mg sodium, 22 g carbo., 3 g fiber, 22 g pro. Daily values: 114% vit. A, 55% vit. C, 14% calcium, 13% iron

# italian greens
# & cheese tortellini

Tender spinach and sugar snap peas team with cheese tortellini in this lemon-scented soup. Sprinkle each serving with fresh Parmesan cheese for a sharp flavor accent.

66

1½ cups finely chopped onion

5 cloves garlic, minced

1 teaspoon dried Italian seasoning, crushed

1 tablespoon olive oil

2 14½-ounce cans reduced-sodium chicken broth

1½ cups water

1 9-ounce package refrigerated cheese tortellini

2 cups sugar snap peas, tips and strings removed, halved crosswise

2 cups shredded spinach

2 teaspoons lemon juice

2 tablespoons finely shredded Parmesan cheese

**Start to finish: 35 minutes   Makes 4 servings (7½ cups)**

In a Dutch oven cook onion, garlic, and Italian seasoning in hot oil over medium heat until onion is tender. Add chicken broth and water. Bring to boiling; add tortellini. Return to boiling; reduce heat. Simmer, uncovered, for 4 minutes.

Stir in snap peas, spinach, and lemon juice. Return to boiling; reduce heat. Simmer, uncovered, for 2 minutes more. Top each serving with Parmesan cheese.

Nutrition facts per serving: 320 cal., 10 g total fat (2 g sat. fat), 33 mg chol., 881 mg sodium, 42 g carbo., 4 g fiber, 17 g pro. Daily values: 21% vit. A, 74% vit. C, 18% calcium, 25% iron

# roasted red pepper soup

Looking for cooking shortcuts? Grab a jar of roasted red sweet peppers and you'll have the beginning of a bright bowl of soup. Serve this rich cream soup with sesame crackers and a cucumber and tomato salad dressed with a light vinaigrette.

**Start to finish: 35 minutes   Makes 5 servings (5½ cups)**

In a large saucepan combine chicken broth, roasted peppers, onion, carrot, celery, sugar, and salt. Bring to boiling; reduce heat. Simmer, uncovered, about 15 minutes or until carrot and celery are very tender. Cool slightly.

Place the pepper mixture, half at a time, in a blender container or food processor bowl. Cover and blend or process until smooth. Return the mixture to saucepan. Stir in half-and-half; cook over medium heat until heated through.

Nutrition facts per serving: 229 cal., 13 g total fat (5 g sat. fat), 23 mg chol., 619 mg sodium, 12 g carbo., 3 g fiber, 6 g pro. Daily values: 68% vit. A, 276% vit. C, 7% calcium, 8% iron

3 **cups chicken broth**

2 **7-ounce jars roasted red sweet peppers, drained and rinsed**

1 **large onion, chopped**

1 **medium carrot, thinly sliced**

1 **stalk celery, thinly sliced**

¼ **teaspoon sugar**

¼ **teaspoon salt**

1¼ **cups half-and-half, light cream, or milk**

# white bean & pasta soup

Perfect for a Sunday night supper on a cool evening, this meatless soup will satisfy even the most demanding appetites. If you have a meat-loving crew, add 1 to 1½ cups chopped cooked chicken along with the beans.

2 cups vegetable broth
  or chicken broth

2 medium carrots, chopped

1 medium onion, chopped

1 stalk celery, sliced

⅛ teaspoon ground white pepper
  (optional)

1 cup dried radiatore or
  mostaccioli

2 cups milk

3 tablespoons all-purpose flour

1 15-ounce can great northern or
  white kidney (cannellini)
  beans, drained and rinsed

1 tablespoon snipped fresh thyme

1 cup chopped tomato

**Start to finish: 35 minutes    Makes 4 or 5 servings (6⅔ cups)**

In a large saucepan combine the vegetable broth, carrots, onion, celery, and, if desired, white pepper. Bring to boiling; stir in pasta. Return to boiling; reduce heat. Simmer, covered, for 10 to 12 minutes or until pasta is tender but still firm.

Meanwhile, gradually stir milk into flour until smooth; stir flour mixture into pasta mixture. Cook and stir over medium heat until thickened and bubbly. Cook and stir for 2 minutes more. Stir in beans and thyme; heat through. Top individual servings with tomato.

Nutrition facts per serving: 340 cal., 4 g total fat (2 g sat. fat), 10 mg chol., 970 mg sodium, 56 g carbo., 7 g fiber, 19 g pro. Daily values: 127% vit. A, 19% vit. C, 20% calcium, 27% iron

# garbanzo bean stew

No need to wait for cooler weather to serve this colorful stew. It is a satisfying meal any time of year. The feta cheese—an optional addition—lends a tangy, fresh flavor.

**Start to finish: 20 minutes   Makes 4 servings (6 cups)**

In a large covered saucepan cook onion, sweet pepper, and garlic in hot oil until onion is tender, stirring occasionally. Stir in cumin, paprika, and ground red pepper; cook for 1 minute.

Carefully add the water, broth, frozen corn, and oregano. Bring to boiling; reduce heat. Simmer, covered, for 5 to 10 minutes or until corn is tender. Stir in beans, tomato, and lemon juice. Heat through. Ladle into serving bowls. Sprinkle each serving with feta cheese (if desired) and green onion. Makes 4 servings.

Nutrition facts per serving: 217 cal., 6 g total fat (1 g sat. fat), 0 mg chol., 672 mg sodium, 38 g carbo., 5 g fiber, 9 g pro. Daily values: 21% vit. A, 89% vit. C, 6% calcium, 28% iron

- 1 large onion, chopped
- 1 medium green sweet pepper, chopped
- 3 cloves garlic, minced
- 2 teaspoons cooking oil
- 1½ teaspoons ground cumin
- ½ teaspoon paprika
- ⅛ to ¼ teaspoon ground red pepper
- 1½ cups water
- 2 cups reduced-sodium chicken broth
- 1 10-ounce package (2 cups) frozen whole kernel corn
- 2 tablespoons snipped fresh oregano
- 1 15-ounce can garbanzo beans, drained and rinsed
- 1 medium tomato, chopped
- 2 tablespoons lemon juice
- ¼ cup crumbled feta cheese (optional)
- 2 tablespoons thinly sliced green onion

# tofu-papaya soup

Papaya and coconut milk lend a mellow sweetness to this refreshing soup, while the gingerroot and cilantro add a spirited flavor. Round out this distinctive soup with a sliced tomato and fresh mozzarella cheese salad and crusty hard rolls.

70

1 tablespoon grated gingerroot

1 clove garlic, minced

1 tablespoon olive oil

3 cups vegetable broth

1 large papaya, peeled, seeded,
    and chopped (about 2 cups)

¼ teaspoon bottled hot
    pepper sauce

½ of a 12-ounce package soft tofu
    (fresh bean curd), drained and
    cut into small cubes

2 teaspoons snipped fresh cilantro

¼ cup unsweetened coconut milk

¼ cup chopped peanuts

2 tablespoons chopped green onion

**Start to finish: 35 minutes  Makes 3 servings (5 cups)**

In a large saucepan cook gingerroot and garlic in hot oil for 2 minutes. Stir in vegetable broth, papaya, and hot pepper sauce. Bring to boiling; reduce heat. Simmer, covered, for 15 minutes.

Stir in the tofu and cilantro. Simmer, covered, for 5 minutes more. Stir in the coconut milk; heat through. Top each serving with peanuts and green onion.

Nutrition facts per serving: 188 cal., 14 g total fat (2 g sat. fat), 0 mg chol., 1,039 mg sodium, 18 g carbo., 2 g fiber, 6 g pro. Daily values: 21% vit. A, 97% vit. C, 3% calcium, 8% iron

## the **papaya** puzzle

Ripe papayas are best eaten raw as a fruit, but slightly green papayas can be cooked as a vegetable and are ideal for stirring into soups. Although the pear-shaped papaya can range in size from 1 to 20 pounds, those found most often in the U.S. usually weigh about 1 pound. When ripe, they have a vivid golden-yellow skin. The flesh is a similar color and is juicy and smooth, with a sweet-tart flavor. The large center cavity is full of tiny black seeds; they are edible but usually are discarded.

# italian fish &
## vegetable soup

When you're in the mood for fish, serve rosemary-scented fish soup. Use any fresh fish that has a firm texture and mild flavor.

**Start to finish: 35 minutes   Makes 4 servings (7½ cups)**

In a large saucepan combine water, undrained tomatoes, cabbage mix, zucchini, celery, onion, wine, bouillon granules, rosemary, bay leaves, and garlic.

Bring to boiling; reduce heat. Simmer, covered, about 10 minutes or until vegetables are crisp-tender. Stir in tomato paste; add fish pieces.

Return to boiling; reduce heat. Simmer, covered, about 5 minutes more or until fish flakes easily with a fork. Remove bay leaves.

Nutrition facts per serving: 153 cal., 1 g total fat (0 g sat. fat), 49 mg chol., 825 mg sodium, 15 g carbo., 4 g fiber, 19 g pro. Daily values: 52% vit. A, 65% vit. C, 8% calcium, 17% iron

**convenience** counts

When you're cooking meals for your family at the end of a busy day, count on convenience products from the supermarket. Buy precut vegetables, such as the coleslaw mix used here or already-cut vegetables for dips. Also check out the salad bar, which many large supermarkets now provide. Fresh spinach, sliced sweet peppers, broccoli flowerets, and shredded carrots are just a few items you'll find on the salad bar.

3¼ cups water

1 14½-ounce can diced tomatoes

1½ cups packaged shredded cabbage with carrot (coleslaw mix)

1 small zucchini, chopped (about 1 cup)

1 stalk celery, chopped

1 small onion, chopped

¼ cup dry white wine or water

2 teaspoons instant chicken bouillon granules

2 teaspoons snipped fresh rosemary

2 bay leaves

2 cloves garlic, minced

¼ cup tomato paste

12 ounces fresh sea bass, orange roughy, haddock, or cod fillets, cut into 1-inch pieces

# tomato-basil soup

This soup is inspired by the cuisine of Northern Italy, where tomatoes and basil are popular ingredients. Try it during the summer months when you can use vegetables and herbs fresh from the garden or farmer's market.

2 medium carrots, finely chopped

2 stalks celery, finely chopped

1 large onion, finely chopped

6 cloves garlic, minced

1 tablespoon olive oil

1 cup water

2 pounds tomatoes, chopped
   (about 6 cups)

½ cup snipped fresh basil or
   2 tablespoons dried basil,
   crushed, plus ½ cup snipped
   fresh parsley

1 teaspoon salt

1 tablespoon balsamic vinegar

**Start to finish: 40 minutes   Makes 4 servings (6 cups)**

In a large saucepan cook carrots, celery, onion, and garlic, covered, in hot oil over medium-low heat for 10 minutes, stirring occasionally. Transfer to a blender container or food processor bowl; add the water. Cover and blend or process until smooth. Return to pan.

Stir in half of the tomatoes, half of the fresh basil or all of the dried basil, and the salt. Bring to boiling; reduce heat. Simmer, covered, for 15 minutes. Remove from heat.

Stir in the remaining tomatoes, the remaining fresh basil or all of the parsley, and the balsamic vinegar; heat through.

Nutrition facts per serving: 145 cal., 5 g total fat (1 g sat. fat), 0 mg chol., 618 mg sodium, 26 g carbo., 6 g fiber, 4 g pro. Daily values: 101% vit. A, 116% vit. C, 5% calcium, 14% iron

# choice
## chowders

# spicy pumpkin
# & shrimp soup

During the week, convenience is key. Here's a way to turn a can of pumpkin into an exciting soup. Just the right blend of ginger, cilantro, allspice, and garlic complement the pumpkin for a terrific flavor.

**75**

**Start to finish: 30 minutes   Makes 4 servings (5¾ cups)**

In a large saucepan cook onions, carrots, cilantro, gingerroot, garlic, and allspice, covered, in hot margarine or butter for 10 to 12 minutes or until vegetables are tender, stirring once or twice.

Transfer the mixture to a blender container or food processor bowl. Add ½ cup of the chicken broth. Cover and blend or process until nearly smooth.

In same saucepan combine pumpkin, milk, and remaining broth. Stir in blended vegetable mixture and shrimp; heat through. If desired, thread additional cooked shrimp on small skewers; top each serving with a spoonful of yogurt, snipped chives, and the skewered cooked shrimp.

Nutrition facts per serving: 222 cal., 9 g total fat (2 g sat. fat), 116 mg chol., 579 mg sodium, 19 g carbo., 5 g fiber, 18 g pro. Daily values: 329% vit. A, 15% vit. C, 12% calcium, 25% iron

## on the thaw

It is unsafe to thaw fish, seafood, or any type of meat at room temperature. Thaw them in one of two ways: 1. The best way to thaw is to place the unopened original container in the refrigerator overnight. 2. Place the wrapped package under *cold* running water until thawed.

2   **medium onions, sliced**

2   **medium carrots, thinly sliced**

1   **tablespoon snipped fresh cilantro**

2   **teaspoons grated gingerroot**

2   **cloves garlic, minced**

½   **teaspoon ground allspice**

2   **tablespoons margarine or butter**

1   **14½-ounce can chicken broth**

1   **15-ounce can pumpkin**

1   **cup milk**

1   **8-ounce package frozen, peeled and deveined cooked shrimp, thawed**

**Additional shrimp in shells, peeled, deveined, and cooked (optional)**

**Plain low-fat yogurt or dairy sour cream (optional)**

**Snipped fresh chives (optional)**

# caribbean clam chowder

Clams combine with sweet potatoes, tomatoes, chile peppers, and a hint of lime and rum to make a soup full of exuberant flavor.

76

½ pint shucked clams
   or one 6½-ounce can
   minced clams

2 cups peeled and cubed sweet
   potatoes (1 to 2 medium)

1 medium onion, chopped

1 stalk celery, chopped

¼ cup chopped red sweet pepper

2 cloves garlic, minced

1½ teaspoons snipped fresh
   thyme or ½ teaspoon
   dried thyme, crushed

1 10-ounce can chopped tomatoes
   and green chile peppers

1 tablespoon lime juice

1 tablespoon dark rum (optional)

**Start to finish: 35 minutes   Makes 4 servings (6 cups)**

Drain clams, reserving juice. Add enough water to clam juice to make 2½ cups liquid. If using fresh clams, chop clams; set aside.

In a large saucepan bring the clam liquid to boiling. Stir in the sweet potatoes, onion, celery, sweet pepper, garlic, and, if using, dried thyme. Return to boiling; reduce heat. Simmer, covered, about 10 minutes or until sweet potatoes are tender.

Mash mixture slightly with a potato masher. Stir in clams, undrained tomatoes, lime juice, rum (if desired), and, if using, fresh thyme. Return to boiling; reduce heat. Cook for 1 to 2 minutes more.

Nutrition facts per serving: 128 cal., 1 g total fat (0 g sat. fat), 19 mg chol., 337 mg sodium, 22 g carbo., 3 g fiber, 9 g pro. Daily values: 141% vit. A, 66% vit. C, 6% calcium, 57% iron

# oyster & corn chowder

If you think a fresh oyster chowder will take too long to make, this soup will surprise you. Buy oysters already shucked from the seafood section of the supermarket. They cook in just 5 minutes to create a creamy jalapeño-spiced chowder.

**Start to finish: 40 minutes   Makes 3 servings (4 cups)**

In a medium saucepan cook onion, sweet pepper, and garlic in hot oil over medium heat until vegetables are tender. Carefully stir in chicken broth, potato or rice, jalapeño peppers, salt, and black pepper. Bring to boiling; reduce heat.

Simmer, covered, about 10 minutes or until potato or rice is nearly tender. Stir in undrained oysters, corn, and oregano. Return to boiling; reduce heat.

Simmer, covered, about 5 minutes or until oysters are plump and opaque. Stir in half-and-half; heat through.

Nutrition facts per serving: 312 cal., 13 g total fat (4 g sat. fat), 57 mg chol., 596 mg sodium, 39 g carbo., 4 g fiber, 13 g pro. Daily values: 26% vit. A, 84% vit. C, 8% calcium, 41% iron

| | |
|---|---|
| 1 | large onion, chopped |
| ½ | cup chopped red sweet pepper |
| 1 | garlic clove, minced |
| 1 | tablespoon olive oil |
| 1 | 14½-ounce can chicken broth |
| 1½ | cups chopped potato or ¼ cup uncooked long grain rice |
| 1 | or 2 fresh jalapeño peppers, seeded and finely chopped |
| | Dash salt |
| | Dash black pepper |
| 8 | ounces shucked oysters with their liquid |
| 1 | cup fresh or frozen whole kernel corn |
| 1 | tablespoon snipped fresh oregano |
| ½ | cup half-and-half or light cream |

## don't let the **heat** get to **you!**

When handling jalapeño peppers or other fresh chile peppers, wear rubber or plastic gloves to prevent skin burns. Disposable plastic gloves are ideal and inexpensive. You can purchase them in pharmacies and paint stores. If skin burns should occur, wash the area well with soapy water. If the juices come in contact with the eyes, flush them with cool water to neutralize the chile pepper oil.

# crab chowder

This winning chowder features the prize of all seafood—crabmeat. It's even more enticing with bouquet garni seasoning—a mixture of several herbs—and a small amount of cream cheese.

- **1 6-ounce package frozen crabmeat or one 6-ounce can crabmeat, drained, flaked, and cartilage removed**
- **1 medium zucchini, cut into 2-inch strips**
- **1 medium red or green sweet pepper, chopped**
- **2 tablespoons margarine or butter**
- **2 tablespoons all-purpose flour**
- **4 cups milk**
- **2 tablespoons sliced green onion**
- **½ teaspoon bouquet garni seasoning**
- **¼ teaspoon salt**
- **⅛ teaspoon black pepper**
- **1 3-ounce package cream cheese, cut up**
- **1 teaspoon snipped fresh thyme**
- **Fresh thyme sprigs (optional)**

**Start to finish: 25 minutes   Makes 4 servings (5 cups)**

Thaw crabmeat, if frozen.

In a medium saucepan cook zucchini and sweet pepper in hot margarine or butter until crisp-tender. Stir in the flour. Add the milk, green onion, bouquet garni seasoning, salt, and black pepper.

Cook and stir over medium-high heat until thickened and bubbly. Add the cream cheese; cook and stir until cream cheese melts. Stir in the crabmeat and snipped thyme; heat through. If desired, garnish each serving with additional fresh thyme.

Nutrition facts per serving: 314 cal., 19 g total fat (9 g sat. fat), 64 mg chol., 844 mg sodium, 18 g carbo., 1 g fiber, 19 g pro. Daily values: 34% vit. A, 36% vit. C, 29% calcium, 8% iron

# southern ham chowder

Southern cooks are renowned for pairing ham with vegetables. In this creamy chowder, smoky bits of cooked ham simmer with yellow squash, red sweet pepper, potato, and green onions.

1½ **cups thinly sliced yellow summer squash or zucchini**

½ **cup chopped red or green sweet pepper**

½ **teaspoon dried thyme, crushed**

1 **tablespoon margarine or butter**

2 **cups water**

1½ **cups chopped potato**

**Dash black pepper**

6 **ounces thinly sliced cooked ham or turkey ham, chopped**

¾ **cup finely chopped green onions**

½ **cup half-and-half or light cream**

**Start to finish: 35 minutes   Makes 3 or 4 servings (5 cups)**

In a large saucepan cook the squash, sweet pepper, and thyme in hot margarine or butter over medium heat about 3 minutes or until squash is tender. Add water, potato, and pepper.

Bring to boiling; reduce heat. Simmer, covered, for 12 to 15 minutes or until potato is tender. Remove from heat. Mash slightly with a potato masher. Stir in ham, green onions, and half-and-half; heat through.

Nutrition facts per serving: 261 cal., 12 g total fat (5 g sat. fat), 45 mg chol., 755 mg sodium, 23 g carbo., 2 g fiber, 16 g pro. Daily values: 28% vit. A, 95% vit. C, 7% calcium, 18% iron

## what's the difference?

Do you know the difference between a chowder and a bisque? A chowder typically is a thick, milk- or cream-based soup that contains a variety of seafood and vegetables. It also describes a thick, rich chunky soup. Chowders often are thickened with potatoes or a roux, a flour and fat mixture. A bisque is a thick, rich, and creamy soup made of puréed shellfish or fish, and, sometimes, meat or vegetables. Traditionally, it is thickened with rice.

# vegetable cheese chowder

Frozen vegetables are the secret to this quick chowder. A little smoked Gouda cheese produces the robust flavor.

**Start to finish: 20 minutes   Makes 4 servings (6 cups)**

In a large saucepan combine the frozen vegetables and water. Bring to boiling; reduce heat. Simmer, covered, about 4 minutes or until vegetables are just tender. Do not drain.

Meanwhile, in a screw-top jar combine ⅔ cup of the milk, the flour, and pepper; cover and shake well. Add to saucepan; add the remaining milk and chicken broth. Cook and stir until thickened and bubbly. Cook and stir for 1 minute more. Add the Gouda cheese; cook and stir over low heat until cheese nearly melts.

Nutrition facts per serving: 370 cal., 20 g total fat (13 g sat. fat), 81 mg chol., 942 mg sodium, 22 g carbo., 3 g fiber, 25 g pro. Daily values: 162% vit. A, 72% vit. C, 52% calcium, 9% iron

1 16-ounce package loose-pack frozen broccoli, cauliflower, and carrots

½ cup water

2 cups milk

⅓ cup all-purpose flour

⅛ teaspoon pepper

1 14½-ounce can chicken broth

1 cup shredded smoked or regular Gouda cheese (4 ounces)

# jalapeño corn chowder

Spectacular and rich, this chowder features the popular Southwestern flavors of corn, jalapeño peppers, and red sweet peppers. Although not a must, crumbled feta cheese sprinkled over each serving adds a salty tang to the soup.

**Start to finish: 20 minutes   Makes 4 servings (5 cups)**

In a blender container or food processor bowl combine half of the corn and the chicken broth. Cover and blend or process until nearly smooth.

In a large saucepan combine the broth mixture and the remaining corn. If using fresh corn, bring to boiling; reduce heat. Simmer, covered, for 2 to 3 minutes or until corn is crisp-tender.

Stir in cooked pasta, milk, roasted peppers, and jalapeño peppers; heat through. If desired, top each serving with feta cheese.

Nutrition facts per serving: 247 cal., 3 g total fat (1 g sat. fat), 5 mg chol., 363 mg sodium, 47 g carbo., 1 g fiber, 11 g pro. Daily values: 10% vit. A, 61% vit. C, 7% calcium, 13% iron

3 cups frozen whole kernel corn or 3 cups fresh corn kernels (cut from 6 to 7 ears of corn)

1 14½-ounce can chicken broth

1¼ cups cooked small pasta (such as ditalini or tiny shell macaroni)

1 cup milk, half-and-half, or light cream

¼ of a 7-ounce jar roasted red sweet peppers, drained and chopped (¼ cup)

1 or 2 fresh jalapeño peppers, seeded and finely chopped

½ cup crumbled feta cheese (optional)

# turkey & wild rice chowder

If you yearn for the nutty flavor of wild rice, but time is short, substitute quick-cooking long grain and wild rice mix, omitting the seasoning packet.

6 ounces cooked smoked turkey sausage links

2 cups milk

1½ cups water

1 medium onion, chopped

½ cup chopped red or green sweet pepper

½ cup frozen whole kernel corn

2 teaspoons instant chicken bouillon granules

2 teaspoons snipped fresh marjoram or ½ teaspoon dried marjoram, crushed

¼ teaspoon black pepper

2 tablespoons all-purpose flour

1½ cups cooked wild or brown rice

**Start to finish: 25 minutes   Makes 4 servings (5¾ cups)**

Cut turkey sausage links in half lengthwise; cut into ½-inch-thick slices. In a large saucepan combine the sausage, 1¾ cups of the milk, the water, onion, sweet pepper, corn, bouillon granules, dried marjoram (if using), and black pepper. Bring to boiling.

Meanwhile, combine flour and remaining ¼ cup milk. Stir into turkey mixture. Cook and stir until thickened and bubbly. Cook and stir for 1 minute more. Stir in the cooked rice and, if using, fresh marjoram; heat through.

Nutrition facts per serving: 236 cal., 7 g total fat (3 g sat. fat), 40 mg chol., 742 mg sodium, 30 g carbo., 2 g fiber, 15 g pro. Daily values: 8% vit. A, 16% vit. C, 15% calcium, 9% iron

### rice for later

When you have the time—and to save time later—cook extra rice and save it. Place cooked rice in an airtight container and store it in the refrigerator for up to 1 week or in the freezer for up to 6 months. Generally, 1 cup of uncooked brown or white rice will yield 3 cups of cooked rice. One cup of wild rice will yield about 2⅔ cups of cooked wild rice.

# roasted garlic turkey chowder

Opt for convenience when you select this chowder. Count on the fresh vegetables, turkey, and basil to round out the roasted garlic flavor.

85

**Start to finish: 30 minutes   Makes 4 servings (6 cups)**

In a large saucepan combine broccoli, carrot, potato, water, and onion. Bring to boiling; reduce heat. Simmer, covered, about 6 minutes or until vegetables are tender. Do not drain.

Stir in milk, turkey, condensed soup, and basil. Cook and stir over medium heat until heated through.

Nutrition facts per serving: 269 cal., 9 g total fat (3 g sat. fat), 53 mg chol., 419 mg sodium, 24 g carbo., 4 g fiber, 22 g pro. Daily values: 53% vit. A, 56% vit. C, 15% calcium, 8% iron

1 cup small broccoli flowerets

1 medium carrot, shredded

½ cup chopped peeled potato
  or ½ cup loose-pack frozen
  diced hash-brown potatoes

½ cup water

¼ cup chopped onion

2 cups milk

1½ cups chopped cooked turkey
  or chicken

1 10½-ounce can condensed
  cream of roasted garlic soup

1½ teaspoons snipped fresh basil

# souper quick simmers

# pesto-vegetable soup

A swirl of basil pesto provides the perfect flavor accent for this vegetable and pasta soup. Pesto can be purchased already prepared at your supermarket or deli.

**Start to finish: 25 minutes   Makes 3 servings (5 cups)**

In a large saucepan cook garlic in hot oil for 30 seconds. Add vegetable broth. Bring to boiling; add pasta. Return to boiling; reduce heat. Boil gently, uncovered, for 6 minutes, stirring occasionally.

Stir in stir-fry vegetables; return to boiling. Stir in arugula and spinach; cook and stir for 2 minutes more. Swirl pesto into each serving.

Nutrition facts per serving: 261 cal., 17 g total fat (1 g sat. fat), 2 mg chol., 1,281 mg sodium, 29 g carbo., 1 g fiber, 7 g pro. Daily values: 63% vit. A, 40% vit. C, 7% calcium, 15% iron

2 cloves garlic, minced

1 tablespoon olive oil

2 14½-ounce cans vegetable broth

½ cup dried ditalini pasta or small shells pasta

1 cup packaged frozen stir-fry vegetables

3 cups torn arugula, torn Swiss chard, or shredded Chinese cabbage

2 cups torn spinach

3 tablespoons pesto

# curried chicken soup

This spiced chicken noodle soup can be ready in just 20 minutes. You can use leftover cooked chicken, or buy a roasted chicken from your supermarket's deli.

5 cups water

1 3-ounce package chicken-flavored ramen noodles

2 to 3 teaspoons curry powder

1 cup sliced fresh mushrooms

2 cups cubed cooked chicken

1 medium apple, cored and coarsely chopped

½ cup canned sliced water chestnuts

**Start to finish: 20 minutes    Makes 5 servings (6½ cups)**

In a large saucepan combine water, the flavoring packet from noodles, and curry powder. Bring to boiling.

Break up noodles. Add noodles and mushrooms to mixture in saucepan; reduce heat. Simmer, uncovered, for 3 minutes. Stir in chicken, apple, and water chestnuts; heat through.

Nutrition facts per serving: 221 cal., 8 g total fat (1 g sat. fat), 54 mg chol., 362 mg sodium, 17 g carbo., 1 g fiber, 20 g pro. Daily values: 1% vit. A, 4% vit. C, 2% calcium, 10% iron

# chicken & rosemary soup

Comfort food? Yes. Ordinary? No. Fresh rosemary, assorted vegetables, chicken, and shredded Parmesan cheese make this cream soup a favorite.

**Start to finish: 25 minutes   Makes 4 servings (5 cups)**

In a large saucepan cook onion in hot oil until tender. Stir in chicken broth and pepper. Bring to boiling.

Meanwhile, stir together milk and cornstarch until smooth. Add milk mixture to broth mixture. Stir in squash, peas, and rosemary. Cook and stir until thickened and bubbly. Reduce heat; cook and stir for 2 minutes more. Stir in chicken and Parmesan cheese; heat through.

Nutrition facts per serving: 412 cal., 18 g total fat (7 g sat. fat), 82 mg chol., 610 mg sodium, 24 g carbo., 3 g fiber, 37 g pro. Daily values: 19% vit. A, 16% vit. C, 36% calcium, 15% iron

1 large onion, chopped

2 teaspoons olive oil or cooking oil

1 cup chicken broth

⅛ teaspoon pepper

3 cups milk

4 teaspoons cornstarch

1 small yellow summer squash or zucchini, quartered lengthwise and sliced

1 cup frozen peas

1½ teaspoons snipped fresh rosemary

2 cups chopped cooked chicken

½ cup finely shredded Parmesan cheese

# turkey tortilla soup

Put a Mexican twist on turkey by combining it with tomatoes, succotash, jalapeño pepper, and cilantro. This bold-flavored soup is thickened with a surprise ingredient—crumbled tortilla chips.

2 teaspoons chili powder

1 teaspoon cooking oil

3 cups chicken broth

1 14½-ounce can Mexican-style
   stewed tomatoes

1 10-ounce package
   frozen succotash

2 cups broken tortilla chips

1 fresh jalapeño pepper, seeded
   and chopped

2 cups chopped cooked
   turkey or chicken

¼ cup snipped fresh cilantro

   Chopped avocado (optional)

**Start to finish: 25 minutes   Makes 4 servings (7 cups)**

In a large heavy saucepan cook the chili powder in hot oil over low heat for 1 minute, stirring frequently. Carefully stir in chicken broth and undrained tomatoes. Bring to boiling.

Stir in succotash, ⅓ cup of the tortilla chips, and the jalapeño pepper. Return to boiling; reduce heat. Simmer, covered, about 10 minutes or until succotash is tender.

Stir in the turkey and cilantro; heat through. Top each serving with remaining tortilla chips and, if desired, avocado.

Nutrition facts per serving: 462 cal., 18 g total fat (4 g sat. fat), 59 mg chol., 1,192 mg sodium, 45 g carbo., 6 g fiber, 32 g pro. Daily values: 16% vit. A, 47% vit. C, 6% calcium, 23% iron

# sesame beef &
# sugar snap pea soup

It only takes a little sesame oil to add an Oriental accent to this soup. The nutty flavored oil works its magic on a colorful combination of sugar snap peas, yellow pepper, green onions, and beef.

91

**Start to finish: 20 minutes   Makes 4 servings (6 cups)**

In a large saucepan combine beef broth, water, snap peas, sweet pepper, green onions, sesame oil, and gingerroot. Bring to boiling; reduce heat. Simmer, covered, for 4 to 5 minutes or until vegetables are crisp-tender. Stir in cooked beef and vinegar; heat through. Serve over rice.

Nutrition facts per serving: 274 cal., 7 g total fat (2 g sat. fat), 49 mg chol., 712 mg sodium, 27 g carbo., 1 g fiber, 23 g pro. Daily values: 2% vit. A, 105% vit. C, 3% calcium, 25% iron

2 14½-ounce cans beef broth

1 cup water

1 cup sugar snap peas, strings
  and tips removed

⅓ cup chopped yellow sweet pepper

⅓ cup thinly sliced green onions

1½ teaspoons toasted sesame oil

1 teaspoon grated gingerroot

8 ounces cooked beef, cut into
  bite-size pieces (about 1½ cups)

2 tablespoons rice vinegar or
  white vinegar

2 cups hot cooked rice

# lemon & scallop soup

Long-stemmed, tiny-capped, and slightly crunchy, enoki mushrooms play an important role in Asian cooking. These elegant mushrooms have a light, fruity flavor. Toss a few into the soup at the last moment, as they will toughen if heated.

12 ounces fresh or frozen bay scallops

5 cups reduced-sodium
   chicken broth

½ cup dry white wine or
   reduced-sodium chicken broth

3 tablespoons snipped fresh cilantro

2 teaspoons finely shredded
   lemon peel

¼ teaspoon pepper

1 pound asparagus spears, trimmed
   and cut into bite-size pieces

1 cup fresh enoki mushrooms
   or shiitake mushrooms

½ cup sliced green onions

1 tablespoon lemon juice

**Start to finish: 25 minutes   Makes 4 servings (7 cups)**

Thaw scallops, if frozen. Rinse well and drain.

In a large saucepan combine the chicken broth, wine, cilantro, lemon peel, and pepper. Bring to boiling.

Add the drained scallops, asparagus, shiitake mushrooms (if using), and green onions. Return just to boiling; reduce heat.

Simmer, uncovered, about 5 minutes or until asparagus is tender and scallops are opaque. Remove from heat. Stir in the enoki mushrooms (if using) and lemon juice. Serve immediately.

Nutrition facts per serving: 153 cal., 2 g total fat (0 g sat. fat), 28 mg chol., 940 mg sodium, 10 g carbo., 2 g fiber, 20 g pro. Daily values: 9% vit. A, 50% vit. C, 3% calcium, 6% iron

# quick cioppino

San Francisco's Italian immigrants are credited with creating the original cioppino (chuh-PEE-noh). This version of the delicious fish stew is very easy to make.

94

1 medium green sweet pepper,
   cut into thin bite-size strips

1 large onion, chopped

2 cloves garlic, minced

1 tablespoon olive oil or cooking oil

2 14½-ounce cans Italian-style
   stewed tomatoes

½ cup water

6 ounces fresh cod fillets, cut into
   1-inch pieces

6 ounces peeled and deveined
   fresh shrimp

3 tablespoons snipped fresh basil

**Start to finish: 20 minutes   Makes 4 servings (5½ cups)**

In a large saucepan cook sweet pepper, onion, and garlic in hot oil until tender. Stir in undrained tomatoes and water. Bring to boiling.

Stir in cod and shrimp. Return to boiling; reduce heat. Simmer, covered, for 2 to 3 minutes or until the cod flakes easily and shrimp turn pink. Stir in the basil.

Nutrition facts per serving: 176 cal., 4 g total fat (1 g sat. fat), 82 mg chol., 819 mg sodium, 19 g carbo., 1 g fiber, 17 g pro. Daily values: 20% vit. A, 67% vit. C, 5% calcium, 13% iron

## is the **catch fresh?**

When buying fresh fish, look for a bright color and a sweet, not fishy smell. If possible, buy a whole fish; then cut it up and store what you don't use. Look for slightly bulging eyes and brightly colored gills. Fish steaks or fillets should be firm and moist. Don't buy fish that is off-color or brown on the edges.

Since most of the shrimp available today has been previously frozen, always check to see if defrosted shrimp is firm and shiny. When purchasing frozen shrimp, make sure it is frozen solidly and has little or no odor, no brown spots, and no signs of freezer burn, indicated by a white, dry appearance around the edges. Frozen shrimp should be thawed overnight in the refrigerator or placed under cold running water. Do not thaw at room temperature.

# endive, ham, & bean soup

Curly endive, often mistaken for chicory, grows in loose heads with lacy, green-rimmed outer leaves that curl at the tips. It is used mainly in salads, but here it is cooked briefly and enjoyed in a tasty bean soup.

**95**

**Start to finish: 25 minutes   Makes 4 servings (6 cups)**

In a large saucepan cook onion, carrot, celery, and garlic in hot oil until tender. Stir in chicken broth, kidney beans, ham, and sage.

Bring to boiling. Stir in curly endive; reduce heat. Simmer, covered, about 3 minutes or just until endive wilts.

Nutrition facts per serving: 226 cal., 6 g total fat (1 g sat. fat), 13 mg chol., 1,281 mg sodium, 33 g carbo., 11 g fiber, 20 g pro. Daily values: 66% vit. A, 10% vit. C, 7% calcium, 18% iron

- 1 medium onion, chopped
- 1 medium carrot, chopped
- 1 stalk celery, chopped
- 2 cloves garlic, minced
- 1 tablespoon olive oil or cooking oil
- 4 cups reduced-sodium chicken broth
- 1 19-ounce can white kidney (cannellini) beans, rinsed and drained
- ⅔ cup chopped cooked ham
- ¾ teaspoon dried sage, crushed
- 3 cups shredded curly endive or Chinese cabbage

# salads are for supper

Mom always told you to eat your greens. She never imagined that salads would grow up, too. They now are complete meals, full of flavor and personality. Innovations in packaged greens and a dramatic increase in fresh produce offerings make these meals a breeze to prepare. Even with time at a premium, you can eat wisely and well. Healthful and alluring, *Quick-Toss Salad Meals* offers a tempting variety of colors, textures, and tastes. So get fresh. Your mom would approve.

mixed
grill

# spicy steak & ranch salad

Steak and onions as you've never seen them before! Grilled sirloin is perked up by Cajun spices before slicing, then arranged on tossed greens and topped with a scattering of crispy French-fried onions. This new version has the makings of an instant classic.

99

**Start to finish: 25 minutes   Makes 4 servings**

In a large nonstick skillet cook French-fried onions over medium-high heat about 2 minutes or until browned, stirring occasionally. Set aside.

Meanwhile, combine Cajun seasoning, lime juice, and garlic; rub over both sides of steak. In the same skillet cook steak over medium heat to desired doneness, turning once. (Allow 6 to 8 minutes for medium rare or 9 to 12 minutes for medium.) Remove skillet from heat; let stand for 10 minutes. Cut steak into thin bite-size slices. If desired, season with salt.

On a large serving platter toss together the salad greens, carrots, and radishes. Arrange steak strips over salad greens. Drizzle dressing over salad. Sprinkle with onions.

Nutrition facts per serving: 310 cal., 13 g total fat (4 g sat. fat), 76 mg chol., 557 mg sodium, 16 g carbo., 3 g fiber, 28 g pro. Daily values: 126% vit. A, 40% vit. C, 5% calcium, 28% iron

½ cup French-fried onions

1 tablespoon Cajun seasoning

1 tablespoon lime juice

1 clove garlic, minced

1 pound boneless beef top sirloin steak, cut 1 inch thick

1 10-ounce package European-style salad greens

2 carrots, cut into thin bite-size strips or peeled into thin strips

½ cup thinly sliced radishes

½ cup bottled fat-free ranch salad dressing

# beef & beet salad
# with fresh basil dressing

It's amazing. Eaters who shy away from cooked vegetables are ever-so-adventurous when the veggies are served cool and crisp in a salad. Case in point is this mélange of sliced beets, carrots, parsnips, and zucchini, fortified with lean strips of beef.

100

6 cups torn mixed salad greens

½ pound lean cooked beef, cut into thin bite-size strips

1 small parsnip, thinly sliced (½ cup)

1 medium carrot, thinly sliced (½ cup)

½ cup sliced zucchini

1 recipe Fresh Basil Dressing

½ of a 16-ounce can (about ¾ cup) julienned beets, well drained

**Start to finish: 25 minutes   Makes 4 servings**

In a large bowl toss together salad greens, beef strips, parsnip, carrot, and zucchini. Pour dressing over salad. Toss lightly to coat. Top with beets.

**Fresh Basil Dressing:** In a small bowl gradually stir ¼ cup buttermilk into ¼ cup mayonnaise or salad dressing. Stir in 1 tablespoon snipped fresh basil or ½ teaspoon dried basil, crushed, and dash pepper.

Nutrition facts per serving: 258 cal., 15 g total fat (3 g sat. fat), 41 mg chol., 245 mg sodium, 11 g carbo., 3 g fiber, 20 g pro. Daily values: 55% vit. A, 26% vit. C, 5% calcium, 20% iron

## cooking with **fresh beets**
Fresh beets from the garden or farmer's market can be successfully substituted for canned with a little extra preparation. Wash the beets, slice off the roots and tops, leaving 1 inch of stem. Then cook, covered, in boiling water for 40 to 50 minutes or until tender. Drain and cool slightly. Peel off the skins and julienne or slice.

# grilled steak & potato salad

Warm cubes of grilled steak and new potatoes, laced with Dijon-style mustard, provide a satisfying contrast to cool lettuce leaves in this do-on-the-grill dinner.

**101**

**Prep: 15 minutes   Grill: 35 minutes   Makes 4 servings**

Place potatoes and water in a foil packet, leaving space for steam to build. Grill potato packet on the rack of an uncovered grill directly over medium coals for 20 minutes. Turn packet over; grill about 15 minutes more or until potatoes are tender.

Add steak to grill when potato packet is turned; grill over medium coals to desired doneness, turning once. (Allow 8 to 12 minutes for medium-rare and 12 to 15 minutes for medium.) Spread steak with 1 tablespoon of the mustard blend during the last 5 minutes of grilling. Remove steak and potato packet from grill; let stand while preparing dressing.

For dressing, in a large bowl combine the remaining 2 tablespoons of the mustard blend, the onion or ranch dip, milk, Worcestershire sauce, and pepper. Drain potatoes and add to dressing; toss lightly to coat. Cut steak into thin bite-size slices.

Line 4 plates with lettuce leaves. Arrange steak slices on lettuce-lined plates. Top each with potatoes and green onions.

Nutrition facts per serving: 375 cal., 13 g total fat (4 g sat. fat), 50 mg chol., 346 mg sodium, 42 g carbo., 2 g fiber, 22 g pro. Daily values: 2% vit. A, 41% vit. C, 3% calcium, 30% iron

1½ **pounds whole tiny new potatoes, quartered**

¼ **cup water**

12 **ounces beef rib-eye steak or beef top sirloin steak, cut 1 inch thick**

3 **tablespoons creamy Dijon-style mustard blend**

¼ **cup dairy sour cream onion or ranch dip**

1 **tablespoon milk**

½ **teaspoon Worcestershire sauce**

⅛ **teaspoon pepper**

**Lettuce leaves**

2 **green onions, thinly sliced**

# steak salad

Turn leftover steak into a spectacular second-day salad that wakes taste buds with red onion, blue cheese, and tarragon dressing. Or, fire up the grill and enjoy the pairing of warm steak with cool, buttery Boston lettuce.

½ cup bottled light red wine vinegar and oil salad dressing

1 tablespoon snipped fresh tarragon or ½ to 1 teaspoon dried tarragon, crushed

½ teaspoon cracked or coarsely ground pepper

2 heads Boston lettuce, separated into leaves

½ pound lean cooked beef, cut into thin bite-size strips

1 cup red or yellow baby pear tomatoes

1 cup broccoli flowerets

½ of a medium red onion, cut into thin slices

¼ cup crumbled blue cheese (1 ounce)

½ cup fat-free croutons

**Start to finish: 25 minutes   Makes 4 servings**

For dressing, combine salad dressing, tarragon, and pepper; set aside.

Line 4 plates with lettuce leaves. Arrange beef, tomatoes, broccoli, and onion on plates. Sprinkle with blue cheese. Drizzle with dressing and top with croutons.

Nutrition facts per serving: 229 cal., 11 g total fat (3 g sat. fat), 42 mg chol., 497 mg sodium, 12 g carbo., 3 g fiber, 21 g pro. Daily values: 16% vit. A, 65% vit. C, 7% calcium, 15% iron

# philly-style
## cheese-steak salad

Cheese steaks are hometown nostalgia fare. Re-create the sweet smell of onions and peppers on the grill, toss them with sirloin strips and a cheesy dressing, and you'll swear you can hear do-wop on the corner.

**Start to finish: 30 minutes   Makes 4 servings**

For pita chips, split pita rounds horizontally to make 4 rounds; cut each into 6 wedges. Place on a foil-lined baking sheet. Bake in 350° oven for 8 to 10 minutes or until crisp. Sprinkle with shredded cheese; bake 2 to 3 minutes more or until cheese melts. Set chips aside.

For dressing, in a blender container or food processor bowl, combine salad dressing and semisoft cheese. Cover and blend or process until smooth. Add milk, 1 tablespoon at a time, to make desired consistency. Set dressing aside.

In a large skillet cook sweet pepper strips and onion in hot oil about 4 minutes or until crisp-tender. Remove from skillet. In the same skillet, cook beef strips over medium-high heat for 2 to 3 minutes or until desired doneness. (Add more oil, if necessary.) Return sweet pepper strips and onion to the skillet, stirring to combine; heat through.

On a large serving platter toss together hot beef mixture and salad greens. Drizzle dressing over salad. Serve with pita chips.

Nutrition facts per serving: 457 cal., 23 g total fat (11 g sat. fat), 74 mg chol., 743 mg sodium, 30 g carbo., 2 g fiber, 30 g pro. Daily values: 28% vit. A, 125% vit. C, 16% calcium, 24% iron

2 pita bread rounds

¾ cup shredded Italian-blend cheeses (3 ounces)

½ cup bottled fat-free creamy peppercorn ranch salad dressing

¼ cup semisoft cheese with garlic and herb

Milk

1 red sweet pepper, cut into thin strips

1 yellow sweet pepper, cut into thin strips

1 small onion, cut into thin wedges

1 to 2 tablespoons olive oil

12 ounces boneless beef top sirloin steak, cut into thin bite-size strips

8 cups torn mixed salad greens

# beef & apple salad

Meal appeal comes from taste, aroma, presentation, and texture, an under-appreciated element that adds snap to a dish. This crunchy example includes crisp raw apples, jicama, and carrots, along with slices of beef.

**Start to finish: 30 minutes   Makes 4 servings**

For dressing, in a screw-top jar combine apple juice, salad oil, and vinegar. Cover and shake well.

Line 4 plates with lettuce leaves. Arrange the apples, beef, jicama, and carrots atop lettuce. Top with cherries. Drizzle dressing over salads. If desired, sprinkle with pepper.

Nutrition facts per serving: 327 cal., 18 g total fat (4 g sat. fat), 33 mg chol., 62 mg sodium, 25 g carbo., 3 g fiber, 19 g pro. Daily values: 106% vit. A, 34% vit. C, 2% calcium, 16% iron

¼ cup apple juice

¼ cup salad oil

2 tablespoons wine vinegar

Lettuce leaves

2 medium apples or pears, cut into wedges

8 ounces lean cooked beef, cut into thin bite-size strips (1½ cups)

1 cup jicama cut into thin bite-size strips

2 medium carrots, cut into thin bite-size strips (1 cup)

¼ cup dried cherries or cranberries, snipped

Coarsely ground pepper (optional)

# beef & curry pinwheels on spinach

Pick up roast beef sliced to your liking at the deli, and the work is half done for this protein-rich entrée. Fresh asparagus is a crisp counterpoint to the curry and chutney cream filling that's spread on the beef slices.

106

1    **pound asparagus spears**

⅓   **of an 8-ounce tub (about ⅓ cup) cream cheese**

3    **tablespoons peach or mango chutney, snipped**

2    **tablespoons finely chopped green onion**

¼   **teaspoon curry powder**

½   **pound lean cooked beef, thinly sliced (about 8 slices)**

6    **cups torn fresh spinach or torn mixed salad greens**

2    **tablespoons lemon juice**

1    **tablespoon olive oil**

2    **tablespoons chopped peanuts**

**Start to finish: 30 minutes   Makes 4 servings**

Snap off and discard woody bases from asparagus. Cook asparagus spears, covered, in a small amount of boiling water for 4 to 6 minutes or until crisp-tender. Drain; set aside.

Meanwhile, in a small bowl stir together cream cheese, chutney, green onion, and curry powder. Spread about 1 tablespoon of the cream cheese mixture over each beef slice. Roll up each beef slice, starting from the short side; cut each beef pinwheel in half.

Divide spinach among 4 plates. Arrange asparagus spears atop spinach. Stir together the lemon juice and olive oil; drizzle over spinach and asparagus. Arrange 4 of the beef pinwheels on each plate; sprinkle with the peanuts.

Nutrition facts per serving: 317 cal., 19 g total fat (6 g sat. fat), 71 mg chol., 213 mg sodium, 16 g carbo., 4 g fiber, 24 g pro. Daily values: 66% vit. A, 76% vit. C, 10% calcium, 31% iron

# pork & pear spinach salad

Fruit, cheese, and nuts are a classic trio with endless intriguing combinations. When you introduce them to savory onions and pork, and dress them all with a mustard-vinegar topping, you have a salad for the ages.

**Start to finish: 25 minutes   Makes 3 servings**

Divide spinach among 3 plates. Arrange pear, pork, and onion on the spinach. Sprinkle with cheese and nuts. Drizzle dressing over salads.

**Mustard Dressing:** In a screw-top jar combine 2 tablespoons olive oil or salad oil, 2 tablespoons vinegar or white wine vinegar, 1½ teaspoons sugar, ¼ teaspoon celery seed, and ⅛ teaspoon dry mustard or ½ teaspoon Dijon-style mustard. Cover and shake well.

Nutrition facts per serving: 331 cal., 22 g total fat (6 g sat. fat), 57 mg chol., 155 mg sodium, 16 g carbo., 4 g fiber, 20 g pro. Daily values: 52% vit. A, 40% vit. C, 9% calcium, 20% iron

*Note: To toast a small amount of nuts, place them in a small skillet. Cook over medium heat, stirring often, for 5 to 7 minutes or until golden.*

4 cups torn fresh spinach

1 medium pear or apple, cored and sliced, or 1½ cups red or green seedless grapes

1 cup cooked lean pork or beef cut into thin strips

½ of a small red or white onion, thinly sliced and separated into rings

1 ounce Brie cheese, cut into thin wedges or cubes, or ¼ cup crumbled blue cheese or feta cheese (1 ounce)

2 tablespoons broken walnuts or pecans or slivered almonds, toasted*

1 recipe Mustard Dressing

# thai cobb salad

Hit a home run with this refreshing mix of meat, cubed avocado, roasted peanuts, and spicy ginger-soy dressing. Leftover grilled meats work admirably, or deli-sliced meats can pinch-hit.

½ cup bottled fat-free Italian salad dressing

1 tablespoon soy sauce

1 to 1½ teaspoons grated gingerroot

¼ to ½ teaspoon crushed red pepper

8 cups torn mixed salad greens*

1½ cups coarsely chopped cooked pork, beef, or chicken (8 ounces)

1 avocado, halved, seeded, peeled, and cut into ½-inch pieces

1 cup coarsely shredded carrots

¼ cup fresh cilantro leaves

¼ cup thinly sliced green onions

¼ cup honey-roasted peanuts (optional)

**Start to finish: 25 minutes   Makes 4 servings**

For dressing, in a large bowl combine dressing, soy sauce, gingerroot, and crushed red pepper. Add salad greens; toss lightly to coat.

Divide salad greens among 4 plates. Top each with meat, avocado, carrots, cilantro, green onions, and, if desired, peanuts.

Nutrition facts per serving: 255 cal., 15 g total fat (4 g sat. fat), 52 mg chol., 743 mg sodium, 11 g carbo., 4 g fiber, 19 g pro. Daily values: 86% vit. A, 19% vit. C, 3% calcium, 13% iron

*Note: To carry through with the Asian flavors, include Chinese cabbage as part of the mixed greens.*

## storing and using fresh ginger

Whole gingerroot stays fresh for two or three weeks in the refrigerator when wrapped loosely in a paper towel, and lasts almost indefinitely when frozen. To freeze, place unpeeled gingerroot in a freezer bag. You can grate or slice the ginger while it's frozen.

# pork salad
# with cabbage slaw

Apples and pork are a can't-miss combination, so this entrée repeats it twice: chopped apples with sliced pork loin and cider vinegar with crumbled bacon. It's a good change of pace, made easy with a base of packaged coleslaw mix.

110

1 pound butterflied pork loin chops, cut about ¾ inch thick

¼ teaspoon cracked black pepper

⅛ teaspoon ground nutmeg

5 cups packaged shredded cabbage with carrot (coleslaw mix)

1 large apple, coarsely chopped

2 slices turkey bacon or bacon

⅓ cup cider vinegar

⅓ cup apple juice or apple cider

1 tablespoon honey

2 teaspoons honey mustard

1 teaspoon caraway seed

**Start to finish: 30 minutes   Makes 4 servings**

Sprinkle chops with pepper and nutmeg. Place on the unheated rack of a broiler pan. Broil 4 to 5 inches from heat for 12 to 15 minutes or until juices run clear and no pink remains, turning once.

Meanwhile, in a large bowl combine cabbage and apple; set aside. Cook bacon in a medium skillet until crisp. Drain; crumble and set aside.

Stir vinegar, apple juice, honey, honey mustard, and caraway seed into skillet. Bring to boiling. Pour over cabbage mixture; add bacon. Toss lightly to coat.

Divide cabbage mixture among 4 plates. Cut chops into ¼-inch-thick slices. Arrange pork slices atop cabbage mixture.

Nutrition facts per serving: 235 cal., 9 g total fat (3 g sat. fat), 56 mg chol., 171 mg sodium, 21 g carbo., 3 g fiber, 19 g pro. Daily values: 78% vit. A, 78% vit. C, 5% calcium, 11% iron

# spinach, ham, & melon salad

Dazzle family and friends with a star-studded main dish. Use cookie cutters to give melon slices pretty shapes that stand out next to vibrant green spinach and ruby red slices of onion. The tangy dressing can be made ahead and chilled.

**Start to finish: 30 minutes   Makes 4 servings**

Use a melon baller to scoop out the cantaloupe pulp into balls.

In a large bowl toss together cantaloupe balls, spinach, ham, pecans, and red onion slices. Pour dressing over salad. Toss lightly to coat.

**Orange-Poppy Seed Dressing:** In a food processor bowl or blender container, combine 3 tablespoons sugar, 1½ teaspoons finely shredded orange peel, 2 tablespoons orange juice, 2 tablespoons vinegar, 1 table-spoon finely chopped onion, and dash pepper. Cover and process or blend until combined. With processor or blender running, slowly add ⅓ cup salad oil in a steady stream through hole or opening in top. Process or blend until mixture is thickened. Stir in 1 teaspoon poppy seed. Cover and chill for up to 1 week. Shake well before using. Makes about ¾ cup.

Nutrition facts per serving: 286 cal., 20 g total fat (3 g sat. fat), 19 mg chol., 507 mg sodium, 19 g carbo., 4 g fiber, 12 g pro. Daily values: 91% vit. A, 119% vit. C, 10% calcium, 24% iron

½ of a small cantaloupe

7 cups torn fresh spinach

1 cup cubed cooked lean ham

½ cup pecan halves, toasted

½ of a medium red onion, thinly sliced

⅓ cup Orange-Poppy Seed Dressing

# BLT salad with crostini

BLTs have been a part of the American food experience for decades, but crostini, savory grilled bread slices topped with tomato and garlic, is a more recent addition to our dining vocabulary and an inspired sidekick to the legendary combo.

113

**Start to finish: 30 minutes   Makes 4 servings**

For dressing, in a blender container or food processor bowl, combine mayonnaise or salad dressing, milk, dried tomatoes, and garlic. Cover and blend or process until tomatoes and garlic are finely chopped. Set dressing aside.

Place bread slices on a baking sheet. Bake in a 450° oven for about 5 minutes or until toasted. Turn slices over; spread with some of the dressing. Bake 3 minutes more; set aside.

Meanwhile, in a large bowl toss together salad greens, chopped tomato, cucumber, cheese, and bacon. Drizzle with dressing; toss lightly to coat. Serve with toasted bread slices.

Nutrition facts per serving: 236 cal., 12 g total fat (5 g sat. fat), 33 mg chol., 913 mg sodium, 22 g carbo., 2 g fiber, 13 g pro. Daily values: 12% vit. A, 31% vit. C, 14% calcium, 10% iron

⅓ cup fat-free mayonnaise dressing or salad dressing

4 tablespoons milk

2 tablespoons chopped oil-packed dried tomatoes, drained

1 clove garlic, minced

12 thin slices baguette-style French bread

6 cups torn mixed salad greens

3 plum tomatoes, seeded and chopped (1 cup)

1 small cucumber, halved lengthwise and thinly sliced

½ cup cubed Muenster or mozzarella cheese (2 ounces)

8 slices turkey bacon, crisp-cooked, drained, and crumbled

# pizza in a bowl

Bread salads are an old-world tradition, updated here to reflect our long love affair with pizza. Premade pizza crusts and packaged salad greens make the prep work child's play: Open packages and toss.

¾  cup bottled fat-free Western or French salad dressing

1  tablespoon snipped fresh basil or oregano or ½ teaspoon dried basil or oregano, crushed

8  cups torn romaine

1  8-ounce package (2) Italian bread shells (Boboli), torn into bite-size pieces

1  cup chopped Canadian-style bacon or pepperoni

1  cup shredded reduced-fat mozzarella cheese or pizza cheese (4 ounces)

**Start to finish: 20 minutes   Makes 4 servings**

For dressing, in a small bowl combine salad dressing and basil or oregano; set aside.

In an extra-large bowl toss together romaine, bread shells, meat, and cheese. Drizzle with dressing; toss lightly to coat.

Nutrition facts per serving: 341 cal., 10 g total fat (1 g sat. fat), 33 mg chol., 1,375 mg sodium, 38 g carbo., 3 g fiber, 25 g pro. Daily values: 47% vit. A, 57% vit. C, 8% calcium, 17% iron

# balsamic-glazed
## springtime lamb salad

Balsamic vinegar, a less-astringent, sweeter member of the vinegar family, makes a memorable glaze for grilled lamb chops. Add fresh early pea pods and mixed greens, and the dish defines the essence of spring.

**115**

**Start to finish: 25 minutes   Makes 4 servings**

For glaze, in a small saucepan bring balsamic vinegar just to boiling. Boil gently, uncovered, about 10 minutes or until vinegar is reduced to ⅓ cup. Set glaze aside.

Meanwhile, place chops on the unheated rack of a broiler pan. Broil 3 to 4 inches from heat for 7 to 11 minutes for medium doneness, turning once halfway through.

Cook peas, covered, in a small amount of boiling salted water for 2 to 4 minutes or until crisp-tender. Drain.

Divide salad greens among 4 plates. Top each with 2 lamb chops and some of the sugar snap peas. Drizzle with glaze; sprinkle with nuts.

Nutrition facts per serving: 516 cal., 21 g total fat (6 g sat. fat), 160 mg chol., 163 mg sodium, 23 g carbo., 4 g fiber, 55 g pro. Daily values: 3% vit. A, 85% vit. C, 7% calcium, 51% iron

1 cup balsamic vinegar

8 lamb loin or rib chops, cut 1 inch thick

3 cups sugar snap peas, ends trimmed

6 cups torn mixed salad greens

¼ cup hazelnuts or coarsely chopped walnuts, toasted

# greek lamb salad with yogurt dressing

When menus become ho-hum, bring drama to the table with the elemental Greek trio of lamb, yogurt, and cucumber. Dried tart cherries make the dish sparkle.

116

- 2 teaspoons snipped fresh rosemary or ½ teaspoon dried rosemary, crushed
- 1 clove garlic, minced
- 8 ounces boneless lamb leg sirloin chops, cut ½ inch thick
- 8 cups torn fresh spinach or torn mixed salad greens
- 1 15-ounce can garbanzo beans, rinsed and drained
- ¼ cup chopped, seeded cucumber
- ½ cup plain low-fat yogurt
- ¼ cup chopped green onions
- ⅛ to ¼ teaspoon salt
- ⅛ teaspoon pepper
- 1 clove garlic, minced
- ¼ cup dried tart cherries or golden raisins

**Start to finish: 30 minutes   Makes 4 servings**

Combine rosemary and 1 clove garlic; rub evenly onto lamb chops. Place chops on the unheated rack of a broiler pan. Broil 4 to 5 inches from the heat for 12 to 15 minutes, turning once halfway through.* Cut lamb chops into thin bite-size slices.

Meanwhile, in a large bowl toss together spinach, garbanzo beans, and cucumber. Divide spinach mixture among 4 plates. Arrange lamb slices atop spinach mixture.

For dressing, in a small bowl combine yogurt, green onions, salt, pepper, and 1 clove garlic. Drizzle dressing over salads. Sprinkle with cherries.

Nutrition facts per serving: 243 cal., 6 g total fat (2 g sat. fat), 36 mg chol., 569 mg sodium, 29 g carbo., 8 g fiber, 20 g pro. Daily values: 80% vit. A, 63% vit. C, 17% calcium, 42% iron

*Note: If desired, grill chops on the rack of an uncovered grill directly over medium coals to desired doneness, turning once halfway through. (Allow 10 to 14 minutes for medium-rare or 14 to 16 minutes for medium.)

# chicken salad grows up

# strawberry-peppercorn
# vinaigrette with turkey

An enduring combination is the mix of hot and sweet. See what the fuss is about with a dressing that combines sweet strawberries and pungent cracked pepper. It gives chicken salad a wake-up call.

**Start to finish: 25 minutes   Makes 4 servings**

Divide mesclun among 4 plates. Top each with turkey, kiwifruit, mushrooms, and tomatoes. Drizzle vinaigrette over salads. Toss lightly to coat.

**Strawberry-Peppercorn Vinaigrette:** In a food processor bowl or blender container, combine 1 cup cut-up fresh or frozen strawberries (thaw frozen strawberries), 2 tablespoons red wine vinegar, and ⅛ teaspoon cracked black pepper. Cover and process or blend until smooth.

Nutrition facts per serving: 251 cal., 8 g total fat (2 g sat. fat), 84 mg chol., 102 mg sodium, 15 g carbo., 5 g fiber, 31 g pro. Daily values: 32% vit. A, 150% vit. C, 21% iron

8 cups mesclun or 6 cups torn romaine and 2 cups torn curly endive, chicory, or escarole

2½ cups cooked turkey or chicken, cut into bite-size strips (12 ounces)

2 cups sliced, peeled kiwifruit and/or sliced carambola (star fruit)

1½ cups enoki mushrooms (3 ounces)

1 cup red cherry tomatoes and/or yellow baby pear tomatoes, halved

1 recipe Strawberry-Peppercorn Vinaigrette

# chicken & pears
# with pecan goat cheese

Goat cheese, also known as chèvre, is a popular selection at the cheese shop, thanks to its distinctive tang that plays so well against fruit, nuts, and the bouquet of garden greens known as mesclun. This salad has them all, plus slices of juicy grilled chicken.

- 8 ounces skinless, boneless chicken breast halves
- ¼ cup olive oil or salad oil
- 2 tablespoons balsamic vinegar
- ¼ teaspoon salt
- ¼ teaspoon pepper
- 1 clove garlic, minced
- ¼ cup finely chopped pecans, toasted
- 1 4-ounce log semisoft goat cheese (chèvre), cut into ¼-inch-thick slices
- 8 cups mesclun
- 2 medium pears or apples, thinly sliced

**Start to finish: 30 minutes   Makes 4 servings**

Rinse chicken; pat dry. Place chicken on the unheated rack of a broiler pan. Broil 4 to 5 inches from heat about 9 minutes or until no longer pink, turning once.* Cut chicken breasts diagonally into thin slices.

Meanwhile, for dressing, in a screw-top jar combine oil, vinegar, salt, pepper, and garlic. Cover and shake well; set aside. Press toasted pecans onto one side of each cheese slice.

Divide mesclun among 4 plates. Arrange chicken, pears, and cheese atop mesclun. Drizzle with dressing.

Nutrition facts per serving: 389 cal., 28 g total fat (7 g sat. fat), 55 mg chol., 337 mg sodium, 18 g carbo., 4 g fiber, 18 g pro. Daily values: 7% vit. A, 15% vit. C, 5% calcium, 12% iron

*Note: If desired, grill chicken on the rack of an uncovered grill directly over medium coals for 12 to 15 minutes or until no longer pink, turning once halfway through.

# grilled chicken & raspberry salad

Let's face it: Skinless, boneless chicken needs a supporting cast to perk it up. Raspberry vinegar, red onion, and fresh raspberries combine with mixed greens to produce a festive dish that doesn't get by on looks alone.

**122**

¼ **cup raspberry vinegar**

3 **tablespoons cooking oil**

½ **teaspoon poppy seed**

¼ **teaspoon salt**

¼ **teaspoon pepper**

1 **pound skinless, boneless chicken breast halves**

6 **cups torn mixed salad greens**

½ **of a small red onion, thinly sliced and separated into rings**

1 **cup raspberries**

**Start to finish: 25 minutes   Makes 4 servings**

For dressing, in a screw-top jar combine raspberry vinegar, oil, poppy seed, salt, and pepper. Cover and shake well; set aside.

Rinse chicken; pat dry. Grill chicken on the rack of an uncovered grill directly over medium coals for 12 to 15 minutes or until no longer pink, turning once halfway through. (Or, place chicken on the unheated rack of a broiler pan. Broil 4 to 5 inches from heat about 9 minutes or until no longer pink, turning once.) Cut chicken diagonally into thin slices.

On a large serving platter, arrange salad greens, onion, and chicken. Drizzle with dressing. Sprinkle raspberries over salad.

Nutrition facts per serving: 244 cal., 14 g total fat (2 g sat. fat), 59 mg chol., 190 mg sodium, 8 g carbo., 2 g fiber, 23 g pro. Daily values: 3% vit. A, 19% vit. C, 3% calcium, 10% iron

# pasta with
# chicken & fruit

Want to bring out the full taste of strawberries? Warm them slightly by mixing with hot pasta, and they'll provide a sweet counterpoint to the tart vinaigrette that dresses crunchy walnuts and chicken strips.

**Start to finish: 25 minutes    Makes 4 servings**

Cook pasta according to package directions; drain well. Rinse with cold water; drain again.

Place mesclun in a large bowl; add pasta. Toss lightly to combine. Add chicken, strawberries, onion slices, walnuts, and Parmesan cheese. Drizzle with dressing. Toss lightly to coat.

Nutrition facts per serving: 288 cal., 12 g total fat (3 g sat. fat), 39 mg chol., 193 mg sodium, 28 g carbo., 2 g fiber, 19 g pro. Daily values: 4% vit. A, 62% vit. C, 10% calcium, 13% iron

- 2 cups dried penne
- 3 cups mesclun or torn fresh spinach
- 5 ounces cooked chicken, cut into bite-size strips (1 cup)
- 1 cup sliced strawberries
- ½ cup sliced red onion
- ⅓ cup coarsely chopped walnuts, toasted
- ¼ cup grated Parmesan cheese
- ½ cup bottled balsamic vinaigrette salad dressing

## the **mix** of **greens** called **mesclun**

In the Piedmont region of Italy and the neighboring Provence region of France, salads of mixed greens, known as mesclun, have a long and proud tradition. Mesclun is any combination of baby lettuces grown and harvested together that represent a variety of flavors, textures, and colors. Various combinations are classics: A Provençal salad is known for chervil, arugula, and endive. Salad niçoise owes its tangy flavor to chicory, cress, and dandelion greens. Americans have embraced the idea of using diverse greens, and the selection in today's produce sections allows you to create your own intriguing mesclun mixes.

# southwestern chicken
# & black bean salad

Fusion cooking conquers two continents in this global collaboration of Caesar dressing
and a Mexican ingredient list of black beans, tortilla chips, chili powder, and cilantro.

**Start to finish: 25 minutes   Makes 4 servings**

In a large bowl combine romaine, black beans, chicken, and tomatoes.

For dressing, in a small bowl whisk together salad dressing, chili powder, and cumin. Pour dressing over salad. Toss lightly to coat. Sprinkle with cilantro and tortilla chips.

Nutrition facts per serving: 295 cal., 10 g total fat (1 g sat. fat), 55 mg chol., 913 mg sodium, 26 g carbo., 9 g fiber, 27 g pro. Daily values: 47% vit. A, 83% vit. C, 9% calcium, 30% iron

10 cups torn romaine

1 15-ounce can black beans, rinsed and drained

1½ cups chopped cooked chicken or turkey (about 8 ounces)

1½ cups red and/or yellow cherry tomatoes, halved

½ cup reduced-calorie bottled Caesar salad dressing

2 teaspoons chili powder

½ teaspoon ground cumin

2 tablespoons snipped fresh cilantro or parsley

½ cup broken tortilla chips

# cool-as-a-cucumber chicken salad

The cool in this dish includes its presentation. Shredded chicken surrounds a mound of cubed melon and vegetables, enhanced by a bracing lime-herb dressing. Just the antidote for a sultry day.

2 cups cubed cantaloupe and/or honeydew melon

1 cup very finely chopped cucumber

1 cup very finely chopped zucchini

¼ cup thinly sliced green onions

⅓ cup lime juice

2 tablespoons salad oil

2 tablespoons water

2 tablespoons snipped fresh cilantro or mint

1 tablespoon sugar

⅛ teaspoon ground white pepper

4 cups shredded leaf lettuce

2 cups shredded cooked chicken (10 ounces)

**Start to finish: 25 minutes    Makes 4 servings**

In a large bowl toss together the melon, cucumber, zucchini, and onions.

For dressing, in a screw-top jar combine lime juice, oil, water, cilantro, sugar, and white pepper. Cover and shake well. Drizzle ½ cup of the dressing over the melon mixture. Toss lightly to coat.

Divide lettuce among 4 plates. Top with melon mixture. Arrange chicken around edges of plates. Drizzle remaining dressing over chicken.

Nutrition facts per serving: 268 cal., 13 g total fat (3 g sat. fat), 68 mg chol., 79 mg sodium, 15 g carbo., 2 g fiber, 24 g pro. Daily values: 41% vit. A, 94% vit. C, 6% calcium, 17% iron

# poached chicken & pasta with pesto dressing

What a clever idea: Cut down on pans used in the kitchen by poaching cubed chicken in the same pot with pasta. Once cooked, they're tossed again with a creamy, herb-flecked dressing quickly made with store-bought pesto and sour cream.

**Start to finish: 30 minutes   Makes 4 servings**

Rinse chicken; pat dry. Cut chicken into 1-inch pieces; set aside.

In a large saucepan cook pasta according to package directions, adding chicken the last 5 to 6 minutes of cooking. Cook until pasta is tender but firm and chicken is no longer pink. Drain pasta and chicken. Rinse with cold water; drain again.

In a large bowl combine pesto and sour cream. Add pasta mixture, chopped vegetables, and tomato. Toss lightly to coat. If desired, sprinkle with nuts.

Nutrition facts per serving: 404 cal., 13 g total fat (1 g sat. fat), 47 mg chol., 183 mg sodium, 43 g carbo., 1 g fiber, 26 g pro. Daily values: 7% vit. A, 61% vit. C, 5% calcium, 15% iron

- 12 ounces skinless, boneless chicken breast halves
- 6 ounces dried wagon-wheel macaroni or rotini
- ¼ cup refrigerated pesto sauce
- ½ cup fat-free dairy sour cream
- 1 cup chopped fresh vegetables, such as red, yellow, or green sweet pepper; broccoli flowerets; zucchini; or cucumber
- 1 small tomato, chopped
- ¼ cup pine nuts or chopped walnuts, toasted (optional)

# sesame chicken
# kabob salad

Kabobs in a microwave? Yes, indeed. Up-to-the-minute with Asian condiments such as sesame oil and plum sauce, these kabobs have real eye appeal teamed with slender enoki mushrooms and red radishes.

1 **pound skinless, boneless chicken breast halves**

1 **recipe Sesame Dressing**

1 **tablespoon bottled plum sauce or chili sauce**

2 **cups chopped red cabbage**

2 **cups sliced bok choy or iceberg lettuce**

16 **fresh pineapple wedges**

16 **sugar snap peas, sliced lengthwise**

½ **cup enoki mushrooms (1 ounce)**

½ **cup cut-up radishes**

**Toasted sesame seed (optional)**

**Start to finish: 30 minutes   Makes 4 servings**

Rinse chicken; pat dry. Cut each chicken breast half lengthwise into 4 strips. Thread 2 of the chicken strips on each of eight 6-inch wooden skewers. Place in a 2-quart rectangular microwave-safe baking dish.

Stir together 2 tablespoons of the dressing and plum sauce; brush over kabobs. Cover dish with waxed paper and microwave on high 2 minutes. Turn kabobs over, rearrange in dish, and brush again with the dressing mixture. Microwave for 2 to 4 minutes more or until chicken is no longer pink.

Meanwhile, combine cabbage and bok choy; divide among 4 plates. Top with kabobs, pineapple, sugar snap peas, mushrooms, and radishes. Drizzle dressing over salads. If desired, sprinkle with sesame seed.

**Sesame Dressing:** In a screw-top jar combine 3 tablespoons salad oil, 3 tablespoons rice or white wine vinegar, 1 tablespoon toasted sesame oil, 1 tablespoon soy sauce, ½ teaspoon dry mustard, and ¼ teaspoon crushed red pepper. Cover and shake well.

Nutrition facts per serving: 323 cal., 17 g total fat (3 g sat. fat), 59 mg chol., 324 mg sodium, 19 g carbo., 3 g fiber, 24 g pro. Daily values: 6% vit. A, 110% vit. C, 6% calcium, 15% iron

# scarlet salad

Beets are such an under-appreciated resource. Give them their due in this variation on a salad niçoise. When beets are combined with colorful asparagus, baby corn, and snow peas, it takes only a little imagination to create stunning arrangements on the plates.

130

12  ounces whole tiny new potatoes, thinly sliced

12  ounces asparagus spears

6  cups torn mixed salad greens

1½  cups chopped cooked chicken (about 8 ounces)

1  14-ounce can baby corn, drained

1  8-ounce can sliced beets, drained

1  cup fresh snow pea pods, strings and tips removed

⅓  cup chopped red onion

¼  teaspoon cracked black pepper

⅓  cup bottled red wine vinaigrette or other vinaigrette salad dressing

**Start to finish: 30 minutes    Makes 4 servings**

In a large saucepan cook potatoes, covered, in a small amount of boiling water for 10 minutes. Meanwhile, snap off and discard woody bases from asparagus. Add asparagus spears to saucepan. Cover and cook for 2 to 4 minutes more or until potatoes are tender and asparagus is crisp-tender. Drain. If desired, cover and chill vegetables for up to 24 hours.

To serve, divide salad greens among 4 plates. Arrange the potatoes, asparagus, chicken, baby corn, beets, and snow pea pods atop greens. Sprinkle with chopped onion and pepper. Drizzle dressing over salads.

Nutrition facts per serving: 355 cal., 14 g total fat (3 g sat. fat), 51 mg chol., 574 mg sodium, 34 g carbo., 6 g fiber, 23 g pro. Daily values: 21% vit. A, 107% vit. C, 9% calcium, 34% iron

### all **lettuces** are not **created equal**
For those raised on iceberg, lettuce is a mild-mannered ingredient. But the rich array of lettuces and greens on the market these days allows cooks to select varieties for color, and piquant and sweet tastes. Consider compact smooth-textured Bibb, light-green Boston, crunchy loaf-shaped Romaine, and red and green leaf lettuce. They mix nicely with specialty greens such as peppery watercress, tangy arugula, bitter radicchio, and colorful Swiss chard. Prewashed and cut greens, packaged in plastic bags, have expanded our choices and sliced salad preparation time to seconds.

# turkey & fruit
## with glazed pecans

Glazed nuts are a cook's trump card, because they can be made in advance and saved for a last-minute flourish. Here, sugared pecans mirror the natural sweetness of berries and nectarines, and perk up chunks of broiled turkey tenderloin.

**Start to finish: 30 minutes   Makes 4 servings**

Rinse turkey; pat dry. Place turkey on the unheated rack of a broiler pan. Broil 4 to 5 inches from the heat for 8 to 10 minutes or until tender and no longer pink, turning once. Cool; cut turkey into bite-size pieces.

In a large bowl toss together turkey, salad greens, nectarines, and strawberries. For dressing, in a small mixing bowl whisk together salad oil, honey, and orange juice. Pour dressing over salad; toss lightly to coat. Sprinkle with pecans.

**Glazed Pecans:** Place 3 tablespoons sugar in a heavy medium skillet or saucepan. Cook, without stirring, over medium-high heat until the sugar begins to melt, shaking skillet occasionally. Reduce heat to low. Stir with a wooden spoon until sugar is golden brown and completely melted. Add ½ cup pecan halves, stirring to coat. Spread the pecans on buttered foil; cool. Break pecans apart.

Nutrition facts per serving: 425 cal., 22 g total fat (3 g sat. fat), 50 mg chol., 54 mg sodium, 35 g carbo., 4 g fiber, 24 g pro. Daily values: 8% vit. A, 71% vit. C, 3% calcium, 13% iron

| | |
|---|---|
| 1 | pound turkey breast tenderloin steaks |
| 6 | cups torn mixed salad greens |
| 1½ | cups sliced nectarines |
| 1½ | cups sliced strawberries |
| 3 | tablespoons salad oil |
| 2 | tablespoons honey |
| 2 | tablespoons orange juice |
| 1 | recipe Glazed Pecans |

# citrusy chicken salad

Brown-skinned jicama tastes like a cross between an apple and a water chestnut. Long used in Mexican cooking, it traverses the globe to add snap to a bright-colored, cumin-flavored salad with Mediterranean credentials.

**Start to finish: 25 minutes    Makes 4 servings**

For dressing, in a small bowl stir together orange juice concentrate, olive oil, vinegar, cumin, and ground red pepper. Set aside.

In a large bowl toss together salad greens, chicken, oranges, jicama, and sweet pepper. Pour dressing over salad; toss lightly to coat.

Nutrition facts per serving: 348 cal., 20 g total fat (3 g sat. fat), 68 mg chol., 73 mg sodium, 20 g carbo., 2 g fiber, 24 g pro. Daily values: 25% vit. A, 162% vit. C, 4% calcium, 16% iron

⅓ cup frozen orange juice concentrate, thawed

¼ cup olive oil

2 to 3 tablespoons white wine vinegar or white vinegar

1 teaspoon ground cumin

⅛ teaspoon ground red pepper

4 cups torn mixed salad greens

10 ounces cooked chicken, cut into bite-size pieces (2 cups)

2 medium oranges, peeled and sectioned

1 cup jicama cut into thin bite-size strips

1 medium red sweet pepper, cut into rings

# lemony asparagus &
# new potatoes with chicken

One brief stop to the produce aisle and another to the deli for chicken hot and fragrant from the rotisserie yield a meal that has overtures of springtime. Lemon peel and thyme add the grace notes.

1 pound whole tiny new potatoes, quartered

12 ounces asparagus spears, cut into 2-inch pieces

2 cups shredded or chopped deli-roasted chicken (10 ounces)

1 tablespoon olive oil or cooking oil

2 teaspoons snipped fresh thyme

1 teaspoon finely shredded lemon peel

¼ teaspoon salt

**Start to finish: 25 minutes   Makes 4 servings**

In a medium saucepan cook potatoes, covered, in a small amount of boiling water for 12 minutes. Add asparagus. Cook, covered, for 2 to 4 minutes more or until potatoes are tender and asparagus is crisp-tender. Drain vegetables; return to saucepan. Add chicken to saucepan.

Meanwhile, for dressing, in a small bowl whisk together the oil, thyme, lemon peel, and salt. Drizzle dressing over chicken mixture; toss lightly to coat.

Nutrition facts per serving: 319 cal., 13 g total fat (3 g sat. fat), 76 mg chol., 199 mg sodium, 27 g carbo., 2 g fiber, 23 g pro. Daily values: 17% vit. A, 49% vit. C, 3% calcium, 24% iron

# chicken & broccoli
## with **creamy** dressing

The smell of bacon cooking is irresistible. Top a robust mixture of broccoli slaw, nuggets of red apple, and chopped chicken with bacon, and watch diners materialize, forks in hand.

**Start to finish: 20 minutes   Makes 4 servings**

For dressing, in a small bowl stir together light mayonnaise dressing and vinegar; set aside.

In a large bowl toss together the broccoli, chicken, and apples. Pour dressing over chicken mixture; toss lightly to coat. Sprinkle with bacon.

Nutrition facts per serving: 327 cal., 18 g total fat (4 g sat. fat), 70 mg chol., 360 mg sodium, 18 g carbo., 4 g fiber, 26 g pro. Daily values: 15% vit. A, 144% vit. C, 4% calcium, 12% iron

| | |
|---|---|
| ½ | cup light mayonnaise dressing or salad dressing |
| 2 | tablespoons cider vinegar |
| 4 | cups broccoli flowerets or packaged shredded broccoli (broccoli slaw mix) |
| 2 | cups chopped cooked chicken (10 ounces) |
| 2 | small red apples, chopped |
| 2 | slices bacon, crisp-cooked, drained, and crumbled, or 2 tablespoons cooked bacon pieces |

## cooked **chicken,** your way

There are several fast ways to prepare cooked chicken for salads. The easiest is to cover boneless or bone-in chicken breasts with water or stock and simmer on a stovetop until cooked through. Boneless breasts also can be broiled in the oven for about 6 minutes per side. If preparing large quantities, consider baking bone-in chicken breasts on a rack, skin side up, in a 350° oven for about 45 to 50 minutes. Use the meat for salads and save the juices, skin, bones, and trimmings to make stock for soup.

# warm **sweet potato,** apple, & **sausage** salad

This main dish conjures up crisp autumn days and a fall bounty of sweet potatoes and apples. Leafy raw spinach provides a nutrient-rich base for a hearty salad that includes spicy turkey sausage.

1 pound sweet potatoes or yams, peeled and cut into ½-inch pieces (3 cups)

1 small onion, cut into thin wedges

2 tablespoons margarine or butter

1 pound cooked smoked turkey sausage, cut diagonally into ½-inch-thick slices

2 medium cooking apples, cut into wedges

½ cup bottled sweet-and-sour sauce

½ teaspoon caraway seed

6 cups torn fresh spinach

**Start to finish: 30 minutes   Makes 4 servings**

In a large skillet cook sweet potatoes and onion in margarine over medium heat about 10 minutes or until tender, stirring occasionally.

Stir in sausage, apples, sweet-and-sour sauce, and caraway seed. Cook, covered, over medium heat about 3 minutes or until apples are tender and sausage is heated through, stirring occasionally. (If mixture seems thick, add water, 1 tablespoon at a time, to make desired consistency.)

Place spinach on a large serving platter. Top with sweet potato mixture.

Nutrition facts per serving: 415 cal., 14 g total fat (3 g sat. fat), 72 mg chol., 196 mg sodium, 50 g carbo., 7 g fiber, 24 g pro. Daily values: 257% vit. A, 89% vit. C, 17% calcium, 31% iron

# cabbage & chicken
# with sesame dressing

Unchain yourself from slicing and dicing. Coleslaw mix provides the crunchy base for this Eastern-inspired meal, redolent of sesame oil, red pepper, and soy sauce.

¼ cup bottled Italian salad dressing

1 tablespoon soy sauce

1 teaspoon toasted sesame oil

⅛ to ¼ teaspoon crushed red pepper

3 cups packaged shredded cabbage
   with carrot (coleslaw mix)

2 cups chopped cooked chicken
   (10 ounces)

2 tablespoons snipped fresh cilantro

1 head Boston lettuce, separated
   into leaves

¼ cup slivered almonds, toasted

**Start to finish: 20 minutes   Makes 4 servings**

For dressing, in a small bowl combine salad dressing, soy sauce, sesame oil, and crushed red pepper. Set aside.

In a bowl toss together cabbage, chicken, and cilantro. Drizzle with dressing; toss lightly to coat.

Line 4 plates with lettuce leaves. Divide chicken mixture among plates. Sprinkle with almonds.

Nutrition facts per serving: 298 cal., 18 g total fat (3 g sat. fat), 68 mg chol., 457 mg sodium, 9 g carbo., 3 g fiber, 25 g pro. Daily values: 45% vit. A, 52% vit. C, 6% calcium, 12% iron

**sesame oil:** a little goes a long way
Toasted sesame oil is a flavoring oil, not a cooking oil, and is used sparingly in recipes because of its strong flavor. (There also is a lighter sesame oil that has very little sesame flavor.) Often, the toasted sesame oil is drizzled on a finished stir-fry dish for a crowning touch. Once opened, it should be kept in the refrigerator to prevent it from becoming rancid, and can be stored for up to a year.

# broiled turkey salad
# with pineapple wedges

Want to intensify the sweet goodness of pineapple? Let it sizzle under a broiler and enjoy its caramelized flavor. Add warm strips of turkey and refreshing jicama for an arresting lineup that goes beyond the usual suspects.

**Start to finish: 25 minutes   Makes 4 servings**

Rinse turkey; pat dry. Spray the unheated rack of a broiler pan with non-stick coating. Arrange turkey and pineapple wedges on rack. Broil 4 to 5 inches from heat for 8 to 10 minutes or until turkey is tender and no longer pink. Turn pineapple once during broiling time. Cool; cut turkey into bite-size strips.

Divide lettuce among 4 plates. Arrange turkey, pineapple, jicama, and carrots atop lettuce.

For dressing, stir together yogurt, pineapple juice, curry powder, and pepper. Drizzle dressing over salads.

Nutritional facts per serving: 221 cal., 4 g total fat (1 g sat. fat), 61 mg chol., 95 mg sodium, 21 g carbo., 2 g fiber, 25 g pro. Daily values: 80% vit. A, 31% vit. C, 8% calcium, 12% iron

1   **pound turkey breast tenderloin steaks**

    **Nonstick spray coating**

12   **fresh pineapple wedges**

6   **cups shredded lettuce**

1   **cup jicama cut into thin bite-size pieces**

1   **cup coarsely shredded carrots**

1   **6-ounce carton tropical- or pineapple-flavored fat-free yogurt**

2   **tablespoons pineapple juice or orange juice**

½   **teaspoon curry powder**

    **Dash pepper**

savvy
seafood

# asian grilled salmon salad

Fennel, one of the oldest cultivated plants, is used whole to spice sausages, crushed for tomato sauces, and often is added to poaching liquids for fish. Here, it is pressed into salmon steaks before grilling, making a toothsome base for dressed vegetables.

**141**

**Start to finish: 25 minutes   Makes 4 servings**

Snap off and discard woody bases from asparagus. Rinse fish; pat dry.

Brush asparagus spears and both sides of salmon lightly with oil. Press fennel seed onto both sides of salmon.

Place salmon on the greased rack of an uncovered grill directly over medium coals. Place asparagus on a piece of heavy foil on grill rack next to salmon. Grill for 8 to 12 minutes or until asparagus is tender and the fish begins to flake easily, turning once halfway through.

Meanwhile, line 4 plates with lettuce leaves. Place salmon atop greens. Arrange asparagus, tomato wedges, and enoki mushrooms around salmon. Drizzle with Asian Dressing.

**Asian Dressing:** In a screw-top jar combine 1 tablespoon salad oil, 1 tablespoon rice vinegar, 1 tablespoon soy sauce, 1 teaspoon toasted sesame oil, ¼ teaspoon sugar, and ¼ teaspoon grated gingerroot or ½ teaspoon chopped pickled ginger. Cover and shake well.

Nutrition facts per serving: 255 cal., 13 g total fat (2 g sat. fat), 31 mg chol., 368 mg sodium, 7 g carbo., 2 g fiber, 28 g pro. Daily values: 14% vit. A, 45% vit. C, 4% calcium, 15% iron

- 1 **pound asparagus spears**
- 4 **6- to 8-ounce salmon fillets or steaks, cut 1 inch thick**
- 1 **tablespoon garlic-flavored oil or olive oil**
- 1 **teaspoon fennel seed, crushed**
- 1 **head Bibb lettuce, separated into leaves**
- 1 **medium tomato, cut into thin wedges**
- 1 **cup enoki mushrooms (2 ounces)**
- 1 **recipe Asian Dressing**

# wilted **sorrel** salad

There's no better way to serve dark, leafy greens than with a quick splash of hot bacon and onion dressing. The unexpected twist is the addition of quickly cooked fish fillets.

1  **pound fish fillets, such as orange roughy, sea bass, or salmon**

**Lemon-pepper seasoning**

4  **slices bacon**

1  **small red onion, sliced and separated into rings**

2  **tablespoons dry sherry**

2  **tablespoons honey**

8  **cups torn sorrel and/or fresh spinach**

**Start to finish: 25 minutes   Makes 4 servings**

Rinse fish; pat dry. Arrange fish in a 2-quart square microwave-safe baking dish; tuck under thin edges. Sprinkle fish with lemon-pepper seasoning. Microwave on high until fish is opaque and flakes easily with a fork. (Allow 3 to 5 minutes for ½-inch-thick fillets and 5 to 7 minutes for ¾-inch-thick fillets.)

Meanwhile, in a large skillet cook bacon over medium heat until crisp. Drain bacon, reserving 2 tablespoons drippings in skillet. Crumble bacon and set aside. Add onion to the reserved drippings in skillet. Cook and stir over medium heat until onion is tender. Stir in sherry and honey. Bring to boiling; remove from heat.

In a large bowl toss together sorrel and bacon. Pour sherry mixture over sorrel mixture; toss lightly to coat. Divide sorrel mixture among 4 plates. Top with fish.

Nutrition facts per serving: 211 cal., 5 g total fat (1 g sat. fat), 66 mg cholesterol, 317 mg sodium, 14 g carbo., 3 g fiber, 27 g pro. Daily values: 76% vit. A, 56% vit. C, 10% calcium, 23% iron

# garden greens
## with swordfish

Firm-fleshed fish, such as swordfish or tuna, slices well after cooking, the better to arrange atop arugula and other greens. They all are complemented by an assertive salad dressing made with roasted sweet peppers, conveniently available in a jar.

**143**

**Start to finish: 30 minutes   Makes 4 servings**

Rinse fish; pat dry. Brush fish with lemon juice. Stir together the Italian seasoning, garlic salt, and pepper; rub over fish. Place fish on the greased, unheated rack of a broiler pan.

Broil 4 inches from heat for 5 minutes. Using a wide spatula, carefully turn fish over. Broil 3 to 7 minutes more or until fish flakes easily with a fork. Cool; cut fish into thin bite-size strips.

Divide salad greens among 4 plates. Top with fish and tomatoes. Drizzle dressing over salads.

**Roasted Pepper Dressing:** In a blender container or food processor bowl, combine ½ of a 7-ounce jar roasted red sweet peppers, drained (½ cup); ¼ cup salad oil; 3 tablespoons vinegar; ¼ teaspoon salt; and dash ground red pepper. Cover and blend or process until nearly smooth. Cover and chill for up to 24 hours.

Nutrition facts per serving: 282 cal., 18 g total fat (3 g sat. fat), 45 mg chol., 374 mg sodium, 6 g carbo., 2 g fiber, 24 g pro. Daily values: 17% vit. A, 104% vit. C, 2% calcium, 13% iron

- 1 pound swordfish or tuna steaks, cut 1 inch thick
- 1 tablespoon lemon juice
- 1 teaspoon dried Italian seasoning, crushed
- ¼ teaspoon garlic salt
- ⅛ teaspoon pepper
- 6 cups torn mixed salad greens
- 12 red and/or yellow baby pear tomatoes or cherry tomatoes, halved
- 1 recipe Roasted Pepper Dressing

# scandinavian shrimp salad

Create a Scandinavian smorgasbord all on one plate with vinaigrette-coated shrimp flanked by rye bread topped with cream cheese and cucumbers. A critical ingredient is dillweed, which is sprinkled atop the bread and snipped into the vinaigrette.

144

12 slices party rye bread or
   12 large crackers

3 tablespoons reduced-fat cream
   cheese (Neufchâtel)

⅓ cup shredded cucumber

⅓ cup thinly sliced red onion

   Fresh dill (optional)

6 cups torn mixed salad greens

12 ounces peeled, deveined,
   cooked shrimp

¼ cup bottled nonfat white wine
   vinaigrette salad dressing

1 tablespoon snipped fresh dill

**Start to finish: 25 minutes   Makes 4 servings**

Spread bread slices with cream cheese; top with cucumber and onion. If desired, sprinkle with dill.

Divide salad greens among 4 plates; top with shrimp. Stir together salad dressing and the 1 tablespoon dill; drizzle over salads. Serve with rye bread slices.

Nutrition facts per serving: 218 cal., 5 g total fat (2 g sat. fat), 174 mg chol., 641 mg sodium, 20 g carbo., 1 g fiber, 23 g pro. Daily values: 12% vit. A, 10% vit. C, 6% calcium, 26% iron

# tossed salad with
# shrimp & oranges

Sautéing shrimp is faster than fast food and a healthful change of pace, particularly when draped over fresh spinach leaves. Serve the shrimp with homemade croutons made from leftover sourdough bread.

2  oranges

Orange juice

12  ounces peeled, deveined shrimp

1  teaspoon snipped fresh rosemary

2  tablespoons white wine vinegar

2  tablespoons salad oil

6  cups torn fresh spinach or torn
mixed salad greens

1  small red onion, thinly sliced and
separated into rings

**Start to finish: 30 minutes   Makes 4 servings**

Finely shred 1 teaspoon orange peel; set orange peel aside. Peel and section oranges over a bowl to catch juices; set orange sections aside. Measure juices and add additional orange juice to equal $\frac{1}{3}$ cup; set orange juice aside.

Rinse shrimp; pat dry. Cook shrimp in boiling, salted water for 1 to 3 minutes or until shrimp turn opaque; drain. Rinse with cold water; drain again. Set shrimp aside.

For dressing, in a small saucepan bring the reserved orange juice and the rosemary to boiling. Remove from heat; stir in the reserved orange peel, vinegar, and salad oil.

In a large bowl toss together spinach, onion rings, orange sections, and shrimp. Pour dressing over salad. Toss lightly to coat.

Nutrition facts per serving: 174 cal., 8 g total fat (1 g sat. fat), 131 mg chol., 216 mg sodium, 10 g carbo., 3 g fiber, 17 g pro. Daily values: 62% vit. A, 88% vit. C, 10% calcium, 30% iron

# shrimp with chipotle vinaigrette

Play beat the clock with sautéed shrimp. Cooking time is less than five minutes, then you can leisurely fiddle with the spicy dressing and serve the shrimp as a warm counterpoint to chilled greens.

**Start to finish: 30 minutes   Makes 4 servings**

In a large skillet cook and stir shrimp in hot oil for 3 to 4 minutes or until shrimp turn opaque. Remove from heat; squeeze lime juice over shrimp. Set shrimp aside for up to 30 minutes to cool slightly.

Meanwhile, for vinaigrette, in a small mixing bowl whisk together the chipotle pepper, tomato juice, salad oil, sugar, and garlic.

To serve, divide salad greens among 4 plates. Top with shrimp and onion. Drizzle with vinaigrette.

Nutrition facts per serving: 159 cal., 8 g total fat (1 g sat. fat), 131 mg chol., 253 mg sodium, 6 g carbo., 3 g fiber, 16 g pro. Daily values: 38% vit. A, 54% vit. C, 6% calcium, 23% iron

| | |
|---|---|
| 12 | ounces peeled, deveined medium shrimp |
| 1 | tablespoon cooking oil |
| 1 | tablespoon lime juice |
| ½ to 1 | teaspoon crushed dried chipotle pepper |
| ⅓ | cup tomato juice |
| 1 | tablespoon salad oil |
| ¼ | teaspoon sugar |
| 1 | clove garlic, minced |
| 8 | cups torn mixed salad greens, romaine, or spinach |
| ½ | cup sliced red onion |

## the **buzz** on **chipotle** peppers

Take ripe red jalapeño peppers, smoke them over wood, dry them, and you have chipotle (chih-POHT-lay) peppers. They are hot, but not as hot as cayenne or crushed red pepper. Crushed chipotle pepper has the same smoky, hot flavor and is sold bottled for convenience. If you can't find bottled crushed chipotle pepper, crush 1 to 2 small whole dried chipotle peppers with a mortar and pestle to get ½ to 1 teaspoon.

# seared scallop
## & spinach salad

Give an old favorite a new lease on life by adding sea scallops to the usual lineup in a bacon-spinach salad. The scallops are dusted with chili powder and red pepper before searing—a guaranteed wake-up call for eaters.

**Start to finish: 30 minutes   Makes 4 servings**

Rinse scallops; pat dry. Set scallops aside. In a large bowl toss together spinach, mushrooms, and carrots; set aside.

In a large nonstick skillet cook bacon over medium heat until crisp. Drain bacon, reserving 1 tablespoon drippings in skillet.

In a medium bowl combine chili powder and ground red pepper; add scallops, tossing lightly to coat.

Cook scallops in reserved bacon drippings over medium heat for 1 to 3 minutes or until scallops turn opaque. Remove scallops from skillet; set aside. Add chutney, water, and mustard to skillet. Cook over medium-high heat until hot and bubbly; spoon over spinach mixture, tossing lightly to coat.

Divide spinach mixture among 4 plates. Top with scallops. Sprinkle with bacon.

Nutrition facts per serving: 160 cal., 4 g total fat (1 g sat. fat), 22 mg chol., 324 mg sodium, 19 g carbo., 5 g fiber, 14 g pro. Daily values: 154% vit. A, 63% vit. C, 13% calcium, 32% iron

½ **pound sea scallops**

8 **cups torn fresh spinach**

2 **cups sliced fresh mushrooms**

1 **cup shredded carrots**

4 **slices bacon, cut into ½-inch pieces**

½ **teaspoon chili powder**

⅛ **to ¼ teaspoon ground red pepper**

¼ **to ⅓ cup chutney, snipped**

¼ **cup water**

1 **to 2 teaspoons Dijon-style mustard**

# scallop stir-fry salad

Spinach and cabbage get a coating of many colors with a sauce containing baby corn, orange juice, and sweet bay scallops. It's a cure for the common meal.

- 2 tablespoons orange juice
- 2 tablespoons reduced-sodium soy sauce
- 1 tablespoon rice wine vinegar or white wine vinegar
- 1 teaspoon sugar
- 1 teaspoon toasted sesame oil
- 12 ounces bay scallops
- 1 cup fresh snow pea pods, strings and tips removed
- 2 tablespoons cooking oil
- 1 medium red sweet pepper, coarsely chopped
- ½ cup sliced green onions
- 1 8-ounce jar baby corn, rinsed and drained
- 2 cups shredded Chinese cabbage
- 2 cups shredded fresh spinach or romaine

**Start to finish: 30 minutes   Makes 4 servings**

Stir together orange juice, soy sauce, vinegar, sugar, and sesame oil; set aside. Rinse scallops; pat dry. Halve pea pods lengthwise. Pour 1 tablespoon oil into a wok or large skillet. Preheat over medium-high heat. Stir-fry scallops in hot oil for 3 to 4 minutes or until scallops are opaque.

Remove scallops from wok. Add remaining oil to wok. Stir-fry pea pods, sweet pepper, and green onions for 2 to 3 minutes or until crisp-tender. Add scallops, corn, and orange juice mixture to wok. Cook and stir about 1 minute or until heated through.

In a large bowl combine cabbage and spinach. Top with scallop mixture. Toss lightly to combine.

Nutrition facts per serving: 171 cal., 9 g total fat (1g sat. fat), 26 mg chol., 421 mg sodium, 10 g carbo., 3 g fiber, 15 g pro. Daily values: 40% vit. A, 113% vit. C, 10% calcium, 21% iron

## scallop selection 101

The smallest scallops on the market are the light pink or tan bay scallops, sometimes known as cape scallops. The larger, white scallops are sea scallops. If only sea scallops are available, you may want to cut them in half before cooking, slicing against the grain.

# curried **crab** salad

Dispel the myth: Not all curries are hot. Packaged curry powder purchased at a grocery store is generally a sweet mixture of as many as 20 spices. It does magical things when mixed in a sauce and added to crabmeat.

**Start to finish: 20 minutes   Makes 3 servings**

In a large bowl combine fresh fruit, crabmeat, and celery; set aside.

For dressing, stir together light mayonnaise dressing, yogurt, milk, and curry powder.

Divide salad greens among 3 plates. Top with crab mixture and drizzle with dressing. If desired, sprinkle with raspberries.

Nutrition facts per serving: 200 cal., 9 g total fat (2 g sat. fat), 58 mg chol., 361 mg sodium, 17 g carbo., 2 g fiber, 14 g pro. Daily values: 21% vit. A, 62% vit. C, 11% calcium, 9% iron

2 cups cut-up fresh fruit (such as pineapple, cantaloupe, honeydew melon, or strawberries)

1 6-ounce package frozen crabmeat, thawed

¾ cup sliced celery

¼ cup light mayonnaise dressing or salad dressing

¼ cup plain low-fat yogurt

2 tablespoons skim milk

½ teaspoon curry powder

4 cups torn mixed salad greens

Fresh raspberries (optional)

# going with
# the grain

# grilled **vegetable** salad with **garlic** dressing

Vegetables, sweet and smoky from the grill, give pasta and cheese a jolt of flavor and color. By doing the grilling ahead, and storing the savory dressing in the refrigerator, this maximum-impact dish is done in the time it takes to simmer pasta.

**Start to finish: 25 minutes  Makes 4 servings**

Halve sweet peppers lengthwise; remove and discard stems, seeds, and membranes. Brush sweet peppers, eggplants, and zucchini with oil. To grill, place vegetables on the grill rack directly over medium-hot coals. Grill, uncovered, for 8 to 12 minutes or until vegetables are tender, turning occasionally. Remove vegetables from grill; cool slightly. Cut vegetables into 1-inch pieces.

Meanwhile, cook pasta according to package directions; drain. Rinse with cold water; drain again. In a large bowl combine pasta and grilled vegetables. Pour dressing over salad. Toss lightly to coat. Stir in cheese; sprinkle with parsley.

**Roasted Garlic Dressing:** In a screw-top jar combine 3 tablespoons balsamic vinegar or red wine vinegar, 2 tablespoons olive oil, 1 tablespoon water, 1 teaspoon bottled roasted minced garlic, ¼ teaspoon salt, and ¼ teaspoon pepper. Cover and shake well.

Nutrition facts per serving: 369 cal., 19 g total fat (6 g sat. fat), 61 mg chol., 317 mg sodium, 40 g carbo., 5 g fiber, 12 g pro. Daily values: 38% vit. A, 113% vit. C, 12% calcium, 18% iron

*Note: If using sunburst or pattypan squash, precook for 3 minutes in a small amount of boiling water before grilling.*

2  red and/or yellow sweet peppers

2  Japanese eggplants, halved
   lengthwise

2  medium zucchini or yellow summer
   squash, halved lengthwise, or
   8 to 10 yellow sunburst or
   pattypan squash*

1  tablespoon olive oil

2  cups dried tortiglioni or rigatoni

1  recipe Roasted Garlic Dressing

¾  cup cubed fontina cheese
   (3 ounces)

1  to 2 tablespoons snipped fresh
   Italian parsley or parsley

# mediterranean
## couscous **salad**

This Mediterranean meal is fast, flavorful, and healthy. A lemon and oregano dressing enlivens feta cheese and vegetables on a bed of quick-cooking couscous.

1¾ **cups water**

1 **cup quick-cooking couscous**

1 **recipe Lemon-Oregano Vinaigrette**

1 **medium red sweet pepper,**
  **chopped**

½ **cup chopped, seeded cucumber**

¼ **cup sliced or chopped pitted**
  **Greek black olives or ripe olives**

¼ **cup crumbled feta cheese**

1 **recipe Pita Chips or crisp crackers**

**Start to finish: 25 minutes   Makes 4 servings**

In a small saucepan bring water to boiling. Remove from heat; stir in the couscous. Let stand, covered, for 5 minutes; fluff with fork.

Place couscous in large bowl. Drizzle vinaigrette over couscous. Cool for 10 minutes. Add sweet pepper, cucumber, and olives; toss to combine. Sprinkle with cheese. Serve with Pita Chips.

**Lemon-Oregano Vinaigrette:** In a screw-top jar combine 3 tablespoons lemon juice; 2 tablespoons olive oil; 1 tablespoon snipped fresh mint or ¼ teaspoon dried mint, crushed; and 1 tablespoon snipped fresh oregano or ¾ teaspoon dried oregano, crushed. Cover and shake well.

**Pita Chips:** Cut 2 pita bread rounds in half horizontally; cut each half into 6 wedges. Arrange wedges in a single layer on a baking sheet. Brush lightly with 1 tablespoon olive oil or spray with nonstick spray coating. Sprinkle with ¼ to ½ teaspoon garlic salt. Bake in a 400° oven for 6 to 8 minutes or until crisp and lightly browned.

Nutrition facts per serving: 392 cal., 14 g total fat (3 g sat. fat), 6 mg chol., 287 mg sodium, 57 g carbo., 8 g fiber, 10 g pro. Daily values: 24% vit. A, 70% vit. C, 10% calcium, 19% iron

# gazpacho pasta salad

The flavors of a famed Spanish soup, gazpacho—a cold soup featuring tomatoes, garlic, vinegar, and cucumber—meet Italian cheese tortellini, and the marriage is a huge success. Crunchy croutons complete the combination.

155

**Start to finish: 25 minutes   Makes 4 servings**

Cook pasta according to package directions; drain. Rinse with cold water; drain again.

In a large bowl combine pasta, tomatoes, cucumber, and capers.

For dressing, in a screw-top jar combine oil, vinegar, mustard, and garlic. Cover and shake well. Pour dressing over salad. Toss lightly to coat.

Line 4 plates with lettuce leaves. Divide salad among lettuce-lined plates. Sprinkle with croutons.

Nutrition facts per serving: 352 cal., 16 g total fat (3 g sat. fat), 30 mg chol., 375 mg sodium, 43 g carbo., 2 g fiber, 12 g pro. Daily values: 9% vit. A, 39% vit. C, 11% calcium, 16% iron

- **1 9-ounce package refrigerated cheese tortellini**
- **2 cups cherry tomatoes, halved**
- **1 cup chopped cucumber**
- **2 tablespoons capers, drained**
- **3 tablespoons olive oil**
- **3 tablespoons white wine vinegar**
- **2 teaspoons honey mustard**
- **1 clove garlic, minced**
- **4 leaf lettuce leaves**
- **1 cup croutons**

## foreign intrigue: **the caper caper**

They're an integral ingredient in tartar sauce, a good foil to cream sauces, and a traditional accompaniment to sliced salmon. What are they? Green capers are unopened flower buds on a bush that's grown primarily in Europe. The buds are packed in a vinegar brine and usually are drained, and sometimes rinsed, before using. Tangy and pungent, they have a flavor that can't easily be substituted.

# caribbean **pasta** salad

Tangy blue cheese provides a snappy comeback to ripe tropical fruits in this refreshing entrée. Lean ham or turkey strips make it a full-fledged meal.

8 ounces dried bow-tie pasta

1 papaya or mango, seeded, peeled, and cut into bite-size chunks (1½ cups)

1 cup pineapple chunks

4 ounces lean cooked ham or cooked smoked turkey, cut into bite-size strips (about ¾ cup)

½ cup chopped red sweet pepper

½ cup sliced green onions

½ cup bottled blue cheese salad dressing

2 tablespoons snipped fresh cilantro

**Start to finish: 25 minutes   Makes 4 servings**

Cook pasta according to package directions; drain. Rinse with cold water; drain again.

In a large bowl combine pasta, papaya, pineapple, ham, sweet pepper, and green onions. Pour salad dressing over salad. Toss lightly to coat. Sprinkle with cilantro.

Nutrition facts per serving: 438 cal., 20 g total fat (4 g sat. fat), 82 mg chol., 688 mg sodium, 51 g carbo., 2 g fiber, 15 g pro. Daily values: 32% vit. A, 121% vit. C, 5% calcium, 21% iron

**tropical** timesavers

One of the happy innovations in the supermarket today is jars of chilled sliced papaya and mango, available year-round. Conveniently peeled and always at the peak of ripeness, they are custom-made for salad meals. In season, sliced nectarines can be called upon.

# prosciutto & melon salad

One of the classic appetizers of all time is the partnership of prosciutto and melon. Expand its horizons with the addition of shredded and chopped vegetables, and appealing ribbed pasta shaped like tiny radiators, called radiatore.

**Start to finish: 25 minutes    Makes 4 servings**

Cook pasta according to package directions; drain. Rinse with cold water; drain again.

In a large bowl combine pasta, tomatoes, yellow summer squash, peas, prosciutto, and basil. Pour salad dressing over salad. Toss lightly to coat.

To serve, fan 3 slices of cantaloupe on each of 4 plates; top with salad.

Nutrition facts per serving: 252 cal., 5 g total fat (0 g sat. fat), 0 mg chol., 308 mg sodium, 43 g carbo., 3 g fiber, 11 g pro. Daily values: 26% vit. A, 90% vit. C, 2% calcium, 16% iron

2 cups dried radiatore

1½ cups coarsely chopped tomatoes (2 medium)

1 cup shredded yellow summer squash or zucchini (1 medium)

½ cup frozen peas

2 ounces prosciutto or cooked ham, chopped (about ⅓ cup)

¼ cup snipped fresh basil

⅓ cup bottled balsamic vinaigrette salad dressing

12 thin slices cantaloupe

# mexican fiesta salad

Prepare this creamy chilled salad in the morning and look forward all day to a hearty, corn-and-bean-studded treat. Lime and cilantro infuse the sour cream dressing.

2 cups dried penne or rotini

½ cup frozen whole kernel corn

½ cup light dairy sour cream

⅓ cup mild or medium chunky salsa

1 tablespoon snipped fresh cilantro

1 tablespoon lime juice

1 15-ounce can black beans, rinsed and drained

3 medium plum tomatoes, chopped (1 cup)

1 medium zucchini, chopped (1 cup)

½ cup shredded sharp cheddar cheese (2 ounces)

**Start to finish: 30 minutes   Makes 4 servings**

Cook pasta according to package directions, adding the corn the last 5 minutes of cooking. Drain pasta and corn. Rinse with cold water; drain again.

Meanwhile, for dressing, in a small mixing bowl stir together sour cream, salsa, cilantro, and lime juice. Set dressing aside.

In a large bowl combine pasta mixture, black beans, tomatoes, zucchini, and cheese. Pour dressing over pasta mixture. Toss lightly to coat. Serve immediately or, if desired, cover and chill for up to 24 hours. (After chilling, if necessary, stir in enough milk to make desired consistency.)

Nutrition facts per serving: 373 cal., 9 g total fat (4 g sat. fat), 19 mg chol., 470 mg sodium, 61 g carbo., 7 g fiber, 20 g pro. Daily values: 15% vit. A, 36% vit. C, 15% calcium, 23% iron

# white beans with tuna

Canned beans eliminate soaking and cooking chores, and this recipe works well with any variety on hand. The tuna and dressing come from the pantry as well, making this a good spur-of-the-moment choice.

1  15-ounce can white kidney beans, black beans, or red kidney beans, rinsed and drained

1  cup thinly sliced celery

⅓  to ½ cup desired bottled creamy salad dressing, such as ranch, garlic, Parmesan, honey Dijon, or Italian

¼  cup finely chopped red onion

1  6½-ounce can chunk white tuna (water pack), drained and broken into chunks

1  head Boston or Bibb lettuce, separated into leaves

2  medium red sweet peppers

2  tablespoons snipped fresh dill

**Start to finish: 20 minutes   Makes 4 servings**

In a medium bowl stir together beans, celery, salad dressing, and onion. Gently stir in tuna. If desired, cover and chill for up to 24 hours.

To serve, line 4 plates with lettuce. Halve sweet peppers lengthwise; remove and discard stems, seeds, and membranes. Cut each pepper half lengthwise into 3 strips. Divide pepper strips among lettuce-lined plates. Spoon bean mixture over pepper strips. Sprinkle with dill.

Nutrition facts per serving: 203 cal., 9 g total fat (1 g sat. fat), 13 mg chol., 349 mg sodium, 20 g carbo., 6 g fiber, 19 g pro. Daily values: 45% vit. A, 122% vit. C, 4% calcium, 13% iron

# texas caviar **salad**

This popular appetizer becomes an entrée with the addition of tomato wedges. Black-eyed peas provide protein, and crushed cumin seeds and jalapeño peppers give the mixture its Lone Star kick.

**Start to finish: 25 minutes    Makes 4 servings**

In a medium skillet cook yellow summer squash, jalapeño peppers, cumin seed, and garlic in hot oil about 8 minutes or until the squash is tender, stirring occasionally. Remove from heat; cool slightly.

In a large bowl toss together squash mixture, black-eyed peas, green onions, vinegar, and cilantro. If desired, cover and chill up to 24 hours.

Before serving, toss tomato wedges into salad.

Nutrition facts per serving: 265 cal., 9 g total fat (1 g sat. fat), 0 mg chol., 521 mg sodium, 38 g carbo., 11 g fiber, 12 g pro. Daily values: 6% vit. A, 36% vit. C, 6% calcium, 8% iron

- 2 cups thinly sliced yellow summer squash
- 1 to 2 jalapeño peppers, seeded and chopped (about 2 tablespoons)
- ½ teaspoon cumin seed, crushed
- 2 cloves garlic, minced
- 2 tablespoons cooking oil
- 2 16-ounce cans black-eyed peas, rinsed and drained
- 2 green onions, sliced
- 2 tablespoons vinegar
- 2 teaspoons snipped fresh cilantro
- 3 medium tomatoes, cut into thin wedges

**peppers:** choose **your** weapon

Peppers carry heat ratings, expressed in Scoville units, to serve as a guide when deciding how fiery a dish will be. Habanero and pequín chilies are at the top of the chart; ancho and poblano chilies are at the mild end. Jalapeños and Anaheim or New Mexican chilies are roughly in the middle. All hot peppers contain oils that can burn eyes, lips, and sensitive skin, so wear plastic gloves while preparing them, and wash your hands and under fingernails thoroughly afterward.

# italian mozzarella salad

Fresh mozzarella is a softer, more delicately flavored cousin of the cheese slathered on pizza. Celebrate its incomparable flavor atop a salad of mixed beans, given spark by a garlicky basil dressing. (Pictured on the cover.)

1 **15-ounce can black beans or garbanzo beans, rinsed and drained**

1 **15-ounce can butter beans or great northern beans, rinsed and drained**

1 **small cucumber, quartered lengthwise and sliced (1 cup)**

2 **red and/or yellow tomatoes, cut into thin wedges**

¼ **cup thinly sliced green onions**

**Basil Dressing or ½ cup bottled oil and vinegar salad dressing**

8 **ounces round- or log-shaped fresh mozzarella or part-skim scamorze**

**Start to finish: 20 minutes   Makes 4 servings**

In a large bowl combine beans, cucumber, tomatoes, and green onions. Add dressing; toss lightly to coat. Cut cheese into thin slices; gently toss with bean mixture.

**Basil Dressing:** In a screw-top jar combine ¼ cup red wine vinegar; ¼ cup olive oil or salad oil; 1 tablespoon snipped fresh basil or 1 teaspoon dried basil, crushed; 1 teaspoon Dijon-style mustard; ¼ teaspoon crushed red pepper; and 1 clove garlic, minced. Cover and shake well. Makes about ½ cup. If desired, chill up to 2 days.

Nutrition facts per serving: 434 cal., 23 g total fat (8 g sat. fat), 32 mg chol., 919 mg sodium, 37 g carbo., 6 g fiber, 27 g pro. Daily values: 16% vit. A, 24% vit. C, 36% calcium, 24% iron

## the allure of **fresh mozzarella**

It's worth seeking out Italian markets, good cheese shops, and well-stocked gourmet delis to find fresh mozzarella. It is much softer, moister, and more elastic than the solid mozzarella that's a staple on pizza. In Italy, it's often served sliced in tomato salads or with fresh fruit for dessert. A similar Italian cheese is scamorze (also spelled scamorza or scamorzo) that's often aged and smoked, but eaten fresh when young, like mozzarella.

# autumn vegetable salad with hot bacon dressing

Fresh, barely cooked Brussels sprouts are astonishingly good, a different creature altogether from the steam-table variety. When mixed with garbanzo beans and carrots, and given the hot bacon dressing treatment, they'll be a regular at the table.

163

**Start to finish: 30 minutes   Makes 4 servings**

Trim stems and remove any wilted leaves from fresh Brussels sprouts; wash. Cut any large Brussels sprouts in half lengthwise. Cook, covered, in a small amount of boiling water for 2 minutes. Add carrots; cover and cook for 8 to 10 minutes more or until vegetables are crisp-tender. (Or, cook frozen sprouts according to package directions, adding carrots the last 8 to 10 minutes of cooking.)

Meanwhile, in a large skillet cook the bacon over medium heat until crisp. Drain bacon, reserving 2 tablespoons drippings in skillet. Crumble bacon and set aside.

Stir vinegar, sugar, and savory into drippings. Bring to boiling; add cooked vegetables and garbanzo beans. Cook and stir for 1 to 2 minutes or until heated through.

In a large bowl toss together romaine and vegetable mixture. Top with crumbled bacon.

Nutrition facts per serving: 275 cal., 12 g total fat (4 g sat. fat), 11 mg chol., 530 mg sodium, 36 g carbo., 12 g fiber, 11 g pro. Daily values: 164% vit. A, 153% vit. C, 11% calcium, 34% iron

2 cups Brussels sprouts or one 10-ounce package frozen Brussels sprouts

1½ cups packaged, peeled baby carrots, halved lengthwise

4 slices bacon

¼ cup wine vinegar

1 tablespoon sugar

1 tablespoon snipped fresh summer savory or basil or ½ teaspoon dried savory or basil, crushed

1 15-ounce can garbanzo beans, rinsed and drained

8 cups torn romaine or torn mixed salad greens

# middle eastern
## bulgur-spinach salad

Bulgur or cracked wheat is a Middle Eastern staple. It's often cooked with lamb, but this vegetarian mélange of grain, fruits, and vegetables is equally satisfying and boasts a preparation that's simplicity itself.

**Start to finish: 30 minutes   Makes 4 servings**

In a medium bowl combine bulgur and boiling water. Let stand about 10 minutes or until bulgur has absorbed all the water. Cool 15 minutes.

Meanwhile, for dressing, in a small mixing bowl stir together yogurt, vinaigrette salad dressing, parsley, and cumin.

In a large bowl combine bulgur, spinach, garbanzo beans, apple, onion, and, if desired, raisins. Pour dressing over salad. Toss lightly to coat.

Nutrition facts per serving: 340 cal., 11 g total fat (2 g sat. fat), 2 mg chol., 673 mg sodium, 53 g carbo., 16 g fiber, 13 g pro. Daily values: 58% vit. A, 55% vit. C, 16% calcium, 40% iron

1 cup bulgur

1 cup boiling water

½ cup plain yogurt

¼ cup bottled red wine vinaigrette salad dressing

2 tablespoons snipped fresh parsley

½ teaspoon ground cumin

6 cups torn fresh spinach

1 15-ounce can garbanzo beans, rinsed and drained

1 cup coarsely chopped apple

½ of a medium red onion, thinly sliced and separated into rings

3 tablespoons raisins (optional)

# toasted barley salad

Rescue barley from its supporting role in vegetable soups and make it the headliner in this cold salad that's studded with butter beans and chopped fruit. By toasting it first, barley's rich, nutty flavor shines through.

166

1½ **cups quick-cooking barley**

2 **cups water**

1 **teaspoon instant chicken bouillon granules**

2 **tablespoons light mayonnaise dressing or salad dressing**

⅓ **cup plain fat-free yogurt**

2 **tablespoons lemon juice or orange juice**

¼ **teaspoon crushed red pepper**

¼ **teaspoon dry mustard**

1 **15-ounce can butter beans, rinsed and drained**

1 **cup chopped apple or one 11-ounce can mandarin orange sections, drained**

⅓ **cup sliced green onions**

**Prep: 25 minutes   Chill: 30 minutes   Makes 5 servings**

In a large skillet cook and stir barley over medium heat about 5 minutes or until toasted and golden brown. Remove from heat.

Carefully stir in water and bouillon granules. Bring to boiling. Reduce heat and simmer, covered, for 10 to 12 minutes or until barley is tender and most of the liquid is absorbed. Remove from heat. Spoon barley into a shallow baking pan and place in the freezer for about 30 minutes.*

For dressing, stir together light mayonnaise dressing, yogurt, lemon juice, crushed red pepper, and dry mustard. In a large bowl stir together barley, beans, apple, and green onions. Stir in dressing.

Nutrition facts per serving: 323 cal., 4 g total fat (0 g sat. fat), 0 mg chol., 302 mg sodium, 63 g carbo., 9 g fiber, 11 g pro. Daily values: 4% vit. A, 18% vit. C, 4% calcium, 15% iron

*Note: If desired, cover and chill the barley for 2 to 24 hours in the refrigerator.*

# italian bread salad

Peasant fare—day-old bread, tomatoes, and onions—becomes a substantial supper fit for any table with well-chosen additions of cheese, basil, and vinaigrette. It's a perfect solution to a bumper crop of sweet, vine-ripened tomatoes.

**Start to finish: 25 minutes   Makes 4 servings**

In a large bowl toss together bread, tomatoes, cheese, basil, and green onions. Drizzle vinaigrette over salad. Toss lightly to coat.

**Red Wine Vinaigrette:** In a screw-top jar combine ¼ cup olive oil; 2 tablespoons red wine vinegar or raspberry vinegar; 1 to 2 cloves garlic, minced; ¼ teaspoon salt; and ¼ teaspoon pepper. Cover and shake well.

Nutrition facts per serving: 383 cal., 22 g total fat (6 g sat. fat), 22 mg chol., 582 mg sodium, 35 g carbo., 1 g fiber, 12 g pro. Daily values: 14% vit. A, 37% vit. C, 17% calcium, 15% iron

5  cups torn bite-size pieces (or 1-inch cubes) day-old Italian or wheat bread

2  cups chopped tomatoes

1  cup cubed fresh mozzarella cheese (4 ounces)

¼  cup thinly sliced fresh basil

¼  cup thinly sliced green onions

Red Wine Vinaigrette or ½ cup bottled red wine vinaigrette salad dressing

# peppered pork
## & apricot salad

Dazzle guests with a main-dish salad whose vibrant colors—bright green, apricot, and black and cream—make a statement on a serving platter. Use quick-cooking pork tenderloin, then slice it into appealing medallions.

**168**

1 **12-ounce pork tenderloin**

1 **teaspoon coarsely ground pepper**

1 **6-ounce package long-grain and wild rice mix**

½ **cup snipped dried apricots**

¼ **cup bottled nonfat Italian salad dressing**

2 **green onions, thinly sliced**

2 **tablespoons frozen orange juice concentrate, thawed**

½ **cup frozen peas**

**Fresh apricots, pitted and sliced (optional)**

### Start to finish: 50 minutes   Makes 4 servings

Place pork on a rack in a shallow roasting pan. Sprinkle the pepper evenly over pork. Roast in a 425° oven about 30 minutes or until a meat thermometer reaches 160°. Remove from oven; cover loosely with foil. Let stand for 10 minutes.

Meanwhile, prepare rice mix according to package directions, adding dried apricots the last 5 minutes of cooking. Spread in a shallow baking pan and cool for 20 minutes.

For dressing, in a small bowl combine salad dressing, green onions, and orange juice concentrate. In a large bowl combine rice mixture and peas; drizzle with dressing. Toss lightly to coat.

Spoon rice mixture onto a large serving platter. Cut tenderloin crosswise into thin slices; arrange slices over rice mixture. If desired, garnish with fresh apricots.

Nutrition facts per serving: 356 cal., 6 g total fat (2 g sat. fat), 61 mg chol., 1,056 mg sodium, 50 g carbo., 2 g fiber, 25 g pro. Daily values: 17% vit. A, 32% vit. C, 27% calcium, 4% iron

*To make ahead: Cover and chill rice mixture and meat slices separately for up to 24 hours. Let stand at room temperature for no more than 30 minutes before serving.*

# brown rice & asparagus salad with shrimp

You've run out of excuses not to serve brown rice—it now comes in a quick-cooking variety that's ready in just 10 minutes. Its nutty flavor combines well with shrimp and asparagus, tempered with sweet-hot mustard and vivid bits of dried tomatoes.

8 ounces asparagus, trimmed and cut into 1½-inch pieces

3 cups cooked brown rice, chilled

8 ounces peeled, deveined, cooked shrimp

3 tablespoons chopped oil-packed dried tomatoes, drained

2 tablespoons sweet-hot mustard

¼ cup sliced almonds, toasted

**Start to finish: 20 minutes   Makes 4 servings**

Cook asparagus, covered, in a small amount of boiling water for 3 to 6 minutes or until crisp-tender. Drain; rinse under cold water.

In a large bowl toss together asparagus, rice, shrimp, and tomatoes. Add mustard; toss lightly to coat. Sprinkle with almonds.

Nutrition facts per serving: 296 cal., 7 g total fat (1 g sat. fat), 111 mg chol., 242 mg sodium, 39 g carbo., 4 g fiber, 18 g pro. Daily values: 7% vit. A, 28% vit. C, 6% calcium, 21% iron

# fire-&-ice rice salad

Refreshing and bracing, this chilled salad plays both sweet and hot. Papaya and honey work with picante sauce and lime juice to bring a complex set of flavors to a canvas of white rice and shrimp.

**Start to finish: 15 minutes   Makes 3 servings**

In a medium bowl combine rice, papaya, and shrimp.

For dressing, in a small bowl combine picante sauce, honey, lime juice, and oil; mix well. Pour dressing over rice mixture; toss lightly to coat. If desired, cover and chill for up to 6 hours.

To serve, line 3 plates with lettuce. Top with salad. Sprinkle with cilantro.

Nutrition facts per serving: 348 cal., 4 g total fat (1 g sat. fat), 74 mg chol., 286 mg sodium, 64 g carbo., 1 g fiber, 13 g pro. Daily values: 15% vit. A, 70% vit. C, 4% calcium, 24% iron

2  cups cooked rice, chilled

1  cup chopped papaya or nectarines

4  ounces peeled, deveined, cooked shrimp, chilled

⅓  cup picante sauce

2  tablespoons honey

2  tablespoons lime juice

2  teaspoons olive oil or salad oil

   Lettuce leaves

2  teaspoons snipped fresh cilantro or parsley

potluck
picks

# antipasto on a stick

Salami, vegetables, and cheesy tortellini are marinated overnight, making this a cinch to fix today for travel tomorrow. Serve slices of crusty bread to catch the drips as you eat your antipasto off of skewers (no serving utensils required).

**Prep: 25 minutes   Chill: 2 to 24 hours   Makes 8 servings**

Fold salami slices in quarters. On 16 short or 8 long wooden skewers, alternately thread salami, tortellini, artichoke halves, olives, pepperoncini, and tomatoes. Place kabobs in a plastic food storage container.

Stir together the ½ cup salad dressing and garlic; drizzle over kabobs. Cover and chill for 2 to 24 hours.

Brush bread slices with additional salad dressing. Place bread slices on the unheated rack of a broiler pan. Broil 4 to 5 inches from the heat for 1 minute or until slices are golden brown. Cool. Serve kabobs with toasted bread slices.

Nutrition facts per serving: 233 cal., 13 g total fat (4 g sat. fat), 31 mg chol., 1,020 mg sodium, 19 g carbo., 2 g fiber, 11 g pro. Daily values: 2% vit. A, 12% vit. C, 4% calcium, 10% iron

*Note: If desired, substitute 1 cup (4 ounces) cubed provolone or mozzarella cheese for the tortellini.*

½ **pound thinly sliced salami or other desired meat**

½ **of a 9-ounce package refrigerated cheese-filled tortellini, cooked and drained (about 40)\***

1 **14-ounce can artichoke hearts, drained and halved**

8 **large pitted ripe olives**

8 **pepperoncini salad peppers**

8 **red or yellow cherry tomatoes**

½ **cup bottled reduced-calorie or nonfat Italian salad dressing**

1 **large clove garlic, minced**

16 **thin slices baguette-style French bread**

**Bottled reduced-calorie or nonfat Italian salad dressing**

# artichoke-dill
## potato salad with chicken

Lift potato salad out of its ho-hum doldrums with marinated artichoke hearts, chopped dill pickle, and attention-getting lemon-pepper seasoning. Add cooked chicken, and it takes center stage on the menu.

3 **pounds whole tiny new potatoes**

1 **cup light mayonnaise dressing
  or salad dressing**

½ **cup chopped onion**

2 **tablespoons chopped dill pickle**

2 **tablespoons wine vinegar**

2 **tablespoons Dijon-style mustard**

1 **tablespoon snipped fresh dill
  or 1½ teaspoons dried
  dillweed, crushed**

1½ **teaspoons lemon-pepper seasoning**

2 **cups chopped, cooked chicken
  (10 ounces)**

2 **6-ounce jars marinated artichoke
  hearts, drained and cut up**

2 **hard-cooked eggs, peeled
  and chopped**

**Prep: 30 minutes   Chill: 4 to 24 hours   Makes 10 to 12 servings**

Cook potatoes, covered, in boiling, lightly salted water 20 minutes or just until tender. Drain. Cool potatoes; cut into bite-size pieces.

Meanwhile, in a very large bowl stir together light mayonnaise dressing, onion, dill pickle, vinegar, mustard, dill, and lemon-pepper seasoning. Gently fold in potatoes, chicken, artichoke hearts, and eggs. Cover and chill for 4 to 24 hours. Stir gently before serving.

Nutrition facts per serving: 320 cal., 14 g total fat (3 g sat. fat), 70 mg chol., 593 mg sodium, 36 g carbo., 2 g fiber, 14 g pro. Daily values: 4% vit. A, 42% vit. C, 3% calcium, 20% iron

**take-along** tips
Transporting salads long-distance isn't a problem when meats, fish, eggs, cheeses, and dairy products are kept thoroughly chilled. Tuck ice packs into an insulated container and begin your journey with a cold salad that has been refrigerated overnight. Serve the salad within 2 hours. For tender mixed green salads, pack the dressing separately and toss right before serving. Ditto for crisp garnishes such as nuts or croutons.

# ginger-peanut pasta salad

This versatile recipe will work with nearly any fresh vegetable that's available and is successful with or without shrimp or chicken. The key elements that give the dish its character are the gingery dressing and the sprinkling of chopped peanuts.

**Prep: 25 minutes   Chill: 2 to 8 hours   Makes 8 servings**

Cook pasta according to package directions. If using the pea pods, add them the last 30 seconds of cooking. Drain pasta and pea pods. Rinse with cold water; drain again.

In a large bowl combine the pasta mixture, desired vegetables, shrimp, green onions, and, if desired, cilantro. Drizzle the dressing over pasta mixture; toss lightly to coat. Cover and chill for 2 to 8 hours.

Just before serving, toss salad and sprinkle with peanuts.

**Ginger Salad Dressing:** In a screw-top jar combine ¼ cup salad oil, 3 tablespoons rice vinegar, 2 tablespoons sugar, 2 tablespoons soy sauce, 1 teaspoon grated gingerroot, and ½ teaspoon chili oil or several dashes bottled hot pepper sauce. Cover and shake well. Chill dressing for up to 3 days. Shake dressing before using.

Nutrition facts per serving: 276 cal., 11 g total fat (2 g sat. fat), 69 mg chol., 395 mg sodium, 31 g carbo., 2 g fiber, 14 g pro. Daily values: 39% vit. A, 64% vit. C, 3% calcium, 19% iron

- 8 ounces dried rotini
- 4 cups mixed cut-up vegetables, such as snow pea pods, kohlrabi, cucumbers, carrots, red or green sweet peppers, and radishes
- 2 cups cooked shrimp or chopped cooked chicken (10 ounces)
- ½ cup sliced green onions
- 3 tablespoons snipped fresh cilantro (optional)
- 1 recipe Ginger Salad Dressing
- ⅓ cup chopped peanuts

# curried chicken salad

Ladies' luncheons have changed and so has chicken salad. Today's version is a riot of color—red grapes, green celery, orange slices—and looks to the East for its flavorings of soy sauce and curry.

176

- **2** medium oranges or one 11-ounce can mandarin orange sections, drained
- **3** cups cubed cooked chicken (about 1 pound)
- **2** cups seedless red grapes, halved
- **1** 8-ounce can sliced water chestnuts, drained
- **1** cup thinly sliced celery
- **⅓** cup light mayonnaise dressing or salad dressing
- **⅓** cup lemon-flavored low-fat yogurt
- **2** teaspoons soy sauce
- **1** teaspoon curry powder

**Prep: 30 minutes** **Chill: 4 to 24 hours** **Makes 6 servings**

If using fresh oranges, peel and slice; halve or quarter each slice. In a large mixing bowl combine oranges, chicken, grapes, water chestnuts, and celery.

For dressing, in a small bowl stir together light mayonnaise dressing, yogurt, soy sauce, and curry powder. Pour dressing over chicken mixture; toss lightly to coat. Cover and chill for 4 to 24 hours.

Nutrition facts per serving: 275 cal., 11 g total fat (3 g sat. fat), 68 mg chol., 299 mg sodium, 22 g carbo., 2 g fiber, 24 g pro. Daily values: 2% vit. A, 50% vit. C, 5% calcium, 10% iron

# italian zucchini salad

Ever seen the beautiful layered vegetables in glass jars sitting on counters at Italian groceries? Bring those artful creations to mind with this striking mixture of vegetables, beans, and prosciutto, bound together with a creamy dressing.

178

- 2 large zucchini and/or yellow summer squash, cut into ¼-inch-thick slices (4 cups)
- 1 15½-ounce can white kidney beans, rinsed and drained
- 1 7¼-ounce jar roasted red sweet peppers, drained and cut into thin strips
- 4 ounces prosciutto, cut into thin strips (1 cup)
- 6 cups torn fresh spinach
- 2 cups torn arugula
- ⅓ cup bottled creamy Italian salad dressing
- ¼ cup light mayonnaise dressing or salad dressing
- 1 cup shredded provolone or fontina cheese (4 ounces)
- ½ cup Italian parsley leaves

**Prep: 30 minutes    Chill: 2 to 24 hours    Makes 8 servings**

In a large bowl combine zucchini, beans, roasted red pepper strips, and prosciutto. Cover and chill for 2 to 24 hours.

Just before serving, add spinach and arugula to zucchini mixture; toss to combine.

For dressing, stir together Italian salad dressing and light mayonnaise dressing; pour over zucchini mixture. Toss lightly to coat. Add shredded cheese and parsley; toss to combine.

Nutrition facts per serving: 221 cal., 15 g total fat (4 g sat. fat), 10 mg chol., 628 mg sodium, 14 g carbo., 5 g fiber, 12 g pro. Daily values: 46% vit. A, 122% vit. C, 15% calcium, 16% iron

# boston bean salad with ham

A mixture of glistening high-contrast beans can look glamorous set off by rings of green onion and pink cubes of ham. The taste recalls time-honored Yankee bean-pot dishes, but the fast prep time puts it squarely in the moment.

**Prep: 20 minutes   Chill: 4 to 24 hours   Makes 8 servings**

In a large bowl combine desired beans, celery, and green onions.

For dressing, whisk together the vinegar, molasses, oil, and mustard. Pour dressing over bean mixture; toss lightly to coat. Cover and chill for 4 to 24 hours, stirring occasionally.

To serve, line a salad bowl or platter with lettuce. Stir ham into bean mixture. Using a slotted spoon, transfer bean mixture to lettuce-lined salad bowl or platter.

Nutrition facts per serving: 311 cal., 10 g total fat (2 g sat. fat), 19 mg chol., 1,144 mg sodium, 39 g carbo., 7 g fiber, 19 g pro. Daily values: 2% vit. A, 18% vit. C, 8% calcium, 26% iron

3 15-ounce cans desired beans, such as navy beans, red kidney beans, or black beans, rinsed and drained

1 cup sliced celery

½ cup thinly sliced green onions

½ cup vinegar

¼ cup molasses

¼ cup salad oil

1 tablespoon Dijon-style mustard

Lettuce leaves

2 cups chopped cooked ham (10 ounces)

# red beans & grains

Eliminate the serving dish by using a crusty round of hearth-baked bread for a salad bowl. Inside are red beans, ham, and quinoa—a bead-shape grain that's loaded with protein. Brown rice can substitute for the quinoa.

**Prep: 30 minutes   Chill: 2 to 24 hours   Makes 10 to 12 servings**

In a large bowl combine ham, quinoa, beans, white rice, tomato, sweet pepper, green onions, parsley, and jalapeño pepper. Pour vinaigrette over rice mixture; toss lightly to coat. Cover and chill for 2 to 24 hours.

Just before serving, cut a 1-inch slice from the top of each loaf of bread. Hollow out bread, leaving a ¼- to ½-inch-thick shell. (Save top slice and remaining bread for another use.) Line each of the bread bowls with lettuce. Spoon salad into bread bowls.

**Peppered Vinaigrette:** In a screw-top jar combine 3 tablespoons olive oil; 3 tablespoons red wine vinegar; 2 cloves garlic, minced; 2 teaspoons snipped fresh thyme or ½ teaspoon dried thyme, crushed; ½ teaspoon ground black pepper; and ¼ teaspoon ground red pepper. Cover and shake well.

Nutrition facts per serving: 333 cal., 9 g total fat (2 g sat. fat), 24 mg chol., 961 mg sodium, 45 g carbo., 5 g fiber, 18 g pro. Daily values: 4% vit. A, 66% vit. C, 7% calcium, 29% iron

- 3 **cups diced cooked ham (about 1 pound)**
- 2 **cups cooked quinoa or brown rice**
- 1 **15-ounce can pinto beans, rinsed and drained**
- 1 **cup cooked white rice**
- 1 **large tomato, chopped (1 cup)**
- 1 **yellow or green sweet pepper, chopped (¾ cup)**
- ¼ **cup thinly sliced green onions**
- ¼ **cup snipped fresh parsley**
- 1 **jalapeño pepper, finely chopped**
- 1 **recipe Peppered Vinaigrette**
- 3 **8-inch round loaves crusty bread (country bread)**

  **Red-tip leaf lettuce**

# muffuletta salad

Bring a bit of New Orleans to any gathering with this do-ahead salad that serves a dozen hungry eaters. The salami, ham, cheese, broccoli, and tomatoes are layered and chilled, then topped with toasted bread cubes, recalling the famed muffuletta sandwiches.

182

- **4** 1-inch-thick slices Italian bread
- **2** tablespoons bottled Italian salad dressing or olive oil
- **1** medium red sweet pepper, cut into strips
- **¾** cup bottled Italian salad dressing
- **½** cup sliced celery
- **½** cup sliced pitted green or ripe olives
- **3** tablespoons snipped fresh basil or oregano
- **6** to 8 cups torn romaine
- **½** pound salami, cut into bite-size strips
- **½** pound lean cooked ham, cut into bite-size strips
- **8** ounces cubed provolone cheese
- **1½** cups broccoli flowerets
- **1½** cups cherry tomatoes, halved

**Prep: 30 minutes   Chill: 4 to 24 hours   Makes 12 servings**

For croutons, brush Italian bread slices with the 2 tablespoons salad dressing. Cut into 1-inch cubes. Spread in a large shallow baking pan. Bake in a 300° oven about 15 minutes or until crisp, stirring once or twice. Cool. Store in an airtight container.

Meanwhile, in a very large bowl combine sweet pepper strips, the ¾ cup salad dressing, celery, olives, and basil. Layer in the following order: romaine, salami, ham, cheese, broccoli, and cherry tomatoes. Cover and chill for 4 to 24 hours.

Just before serving, add croutons to salad; toss lightly to coat.

Nutrition facts per serving: 299 cal., 22 g total fat (7 g sat. fat), 38 mg chol., 1,133 mg sodium, 11 g carbo., 2 g fiber, 15 g pro. Daily values: 22% vit. A, 63% vit. C, 14% calcium, 10% iron

# two-bean & rice salad

When you need to feed a crowd, consider this pleaser that easily can be doubled to serve 30. Pinto beans and black beans provide color contrast, and garlic dressing and diced chili peppers give it verve.

**Prep: 25 minutes    Chill: 2 to 24 hours    Makes 16 servings**

In a large mixing bowl combine rice, beans, peas, celery, onion, peppers, and cilantro.

Pour dressing over the rice mixture; toss lightly to coat. Cover and chill for 2 to 24 hours.

**Garlic Dressing:** In a screw-top jar combine $\frac{1}{3}$ cup white wine vinegar, $\frac{1}{4}$ cup olive oil or salad oil, 2 tablespoons water, $\frac{3}{4}$ teaspoon salt, $\frac{1}{2}$ teaspoon garlic powder, and $\frac{1}{2}$ teaspoon pepper. Cover and shake well.

Nutrition facts per serving: 244 cal., 7 g total fat (1 g sat. fat), 0 mg chol., 591 mg sodium, 39 g carbo., 7 g fiber, 9 g pro. Daily values: 2% vit. A, 27% vit. C, 5% calcium, 19% iron

3 cups cooked rice, chilled

1 15-ounce can pinto beans, rinsed and drained

1 15-ounce can black beans, rinsed and drained

1 10-ounce package frozen peas, thawed

1 cup sliced celery

$\frac{1}{2}$ cup chopped red onion

2 medium fresh Anaheim peppers, chopped, or two 4-ounce cans diced green chili peppers, drained

$\frac{1}{4}$ cup snipped fresh cilantro or parsley

1 recipe Garlic Dressing or $\frac{2}{3}$ cup bottled Italian salad dressing

# three-cheese orzo salad

Orzo is pasta shaped like rice that cooks in less than 10 minutes. It's a useful base for vegetables, and, like all pastas, was born to be served with cheese. Make it a triple indulgence with feta, mozzarella, and Parmesan.

2 cups sugar snap peas, ends trimmed

1¼ cups orzo

1 6-ounce jar marinated artichoke hearts

2 cups red or yellow cherry tomatoes and/or baby pear tomatoes, halved

1 cup cubed mozzarella cheese (4 ounces)

1 4-ounce package crumbled feta or peppercorn feta cheese (1 cup)

¼ cup shredded Parmesan cheese (1 ounce)

¼ cup white wine vinegar

¼ cup water

2 teaspoons sugar

1 tablespoon snipped fresh dill or 1 teaspoon dried dillweed

**Prep: 30 minutes   Chill: 4 to 24 hours   Makes 8 servings**

Cook sugar snap peas in a large saucepan of boiling, lightly salted water for 1 minute. Using a slotted spoon, transfer peas to a colander. Rinse under cold water; drain and set aside.

Add orzo to the same saucepan. Boil for 8 to 10 minutes or until tender but firm; drain. Rinse with cold water; drain again.

Meanwhile, drain artichoke hearts, reserving marinade. Cut artichokes into bite-size pieces. In a large bowl toss together artichokes, sugar snap peas, orzo, tomatoes, and cheeses.

For dressing, in a screw-top jar combine reserved artichoke marinade, vinegar, water, sugar, and dill. Cover and shake well. Pour dressing over salad. Toss lightly to coat. Cover and chill for 4 to 24 hours.

Nutrition facts per serving: 233 cal., 8 g total fat (4 g sat. fat), 23 mg chol., 336 mg sodium, 28 g carbo., 1 g fiber, 12 g pro. Daily values: 9% vit. A, 38% vit. C, 17% calcium, 13% iron

**187**

**189**

## METRIC COOKING HINTS

**By making a few conversions,** cooks in Australia, Canada, and the United Kingdom can use the recipes in *Quick Soups, Simple Salads* with confidence. The charts on this page provide a guide for converting measurements from the U.S. customary system, which is used throughout this book, to the imperial and metric systems. There also is a conversion table for oven temperatures to accommodate the differences in oven calibrations.

**Product Differences:** Most of the ingredients called for in the recipes in this book are available in English-speaking countries. However, some are known by different names. Here are some common U.S. American ingredients and their possible counterparts:
- Sugar is granulated or castor sugar.
- Powdered sugar is icing sugar.
- All-purpose flour is plain household flour or white flour. When self-rising flour is used in place of all-purpose flour in a recipe that calls for leavening, omit the leavening agent (baking soda or baking powder) and salt.
- Light-colored corn syrup is golden syrup.
- Cornstarch is cornflour.
- Baking soda is bicarbonate of soda.
- Vanilla is vanilla essence.
- Green, red, or yellow sweet peppers are capsicums.
- Golden raisins are sultanas.

**Volume and Weight:** U.S. Americans traditionally use cup measures for liquid and solid ingredients. The chart, above right, shows the approximate imperial and metric equivalents. If you are accustomed to weighing solid ingredients, the following approximate equivalents will be helpful.
- 1 cup butter, castor sugar, or rice = 8 ounces = about 230 grams
- 1 cup flour = 4 ounces = about 115 grams
- 1 cup icing sugar = 5 ounces = about 140 grams

Spoon measures are used for smaller amounts of ingredients. Although the size of the tablespoon varies slightly in different countries, for practical purposes and for recipes in this book, a straight substitution is all that's necessary.

Measurements made using cups or spoons always should be level unless stated otherwise.

### Equivalents: U.S. = Australia/U.K.

⅛ teaspoon = 1 ml
¼ teaspoon = 1.25 ml
½ teaspoon = 2.5 ml
1 teaspoon = 5 ml
1 tablespoon = 15 ml
1 fluid ounce = 30 ml
¼ cup = 60 ml
⅓ cup = 80 ml
½ cup = 120 ml
⅔ cup = 160 ml
¾ cup = 180 ml
1 cup = 240 ml
2 cups = 475 ml
1 quart = 1 liter
½ inch = 1.25 cm
1 inch = 2.5 cm

### Baking Pan Sizes

| U.S. American | Metric |
| --- | --- |
| 8×1½-inch round baking pan | 20×4-cm cake tin |
| 9×1½-inch round baking pan | 23×4-cm cake tin |
| 11×7×1½-inch baking pan | 28×18×4-cm baking tin |
| 13×9×2-inch baking pan | 32×23×5-cm baking tin |
| 2-quart rectangular baking dish | 28×18×4-cm baking tin |
| 15×10×1-inch baking pan | 38×24×2.5-cm baking tin (Swiss roll tin) |
| 9-inch pie plate | 22×4- or 23×4-cm pie plate |
| 7- or 8-inch springform pan | 18- or 20-cm springform or loose-bottom cake tin |
| 9×5×3-inch loaf pan | 23×13×8-cm or 2-pound narrow loaf tin or pâté tin |
| 1½-quart casserole | 1.5-liter casserole |
| 2-quart casserole | 2-liter casserole |

### Oven Temperature Equivalents

| Fahrenheit Setting | Celsius Setting* | Gas Setting |
| --- | --- | --- |
| 300°F | 150°C | Gas Mark 2 (slow) |
| 325°F | 160°C | Gas Mark 3 (moderately slow) |
| 350°F | 180°C | Gas Mark 4 (moderate) |
| 375°F | 190°C | Gas Mark 5 (moderately hot) |
| 400°F | 200°C | Gas Mark 6 (hot) |
| 425°F | 220°C | Gas Mark 7 (hot) |
| 450° | 230°C | Gas Mark 8 (very hot) |
| 475° | 240°C | Gas Mark 9 (very hot) |
| Broil | | Grill |

*Electric and gas ovens may be calibrated using Celsius. However, for an electric oven, increase the Celsius setting 10 to 20 degrees when cooking above 160°C. For convection or forced-air ovens (gas or electric), lower the temperature setting 10°C when cooking at all heat levels.

add your own recipes

recipe
_____

recipe
_____